EP 65.00 4/99

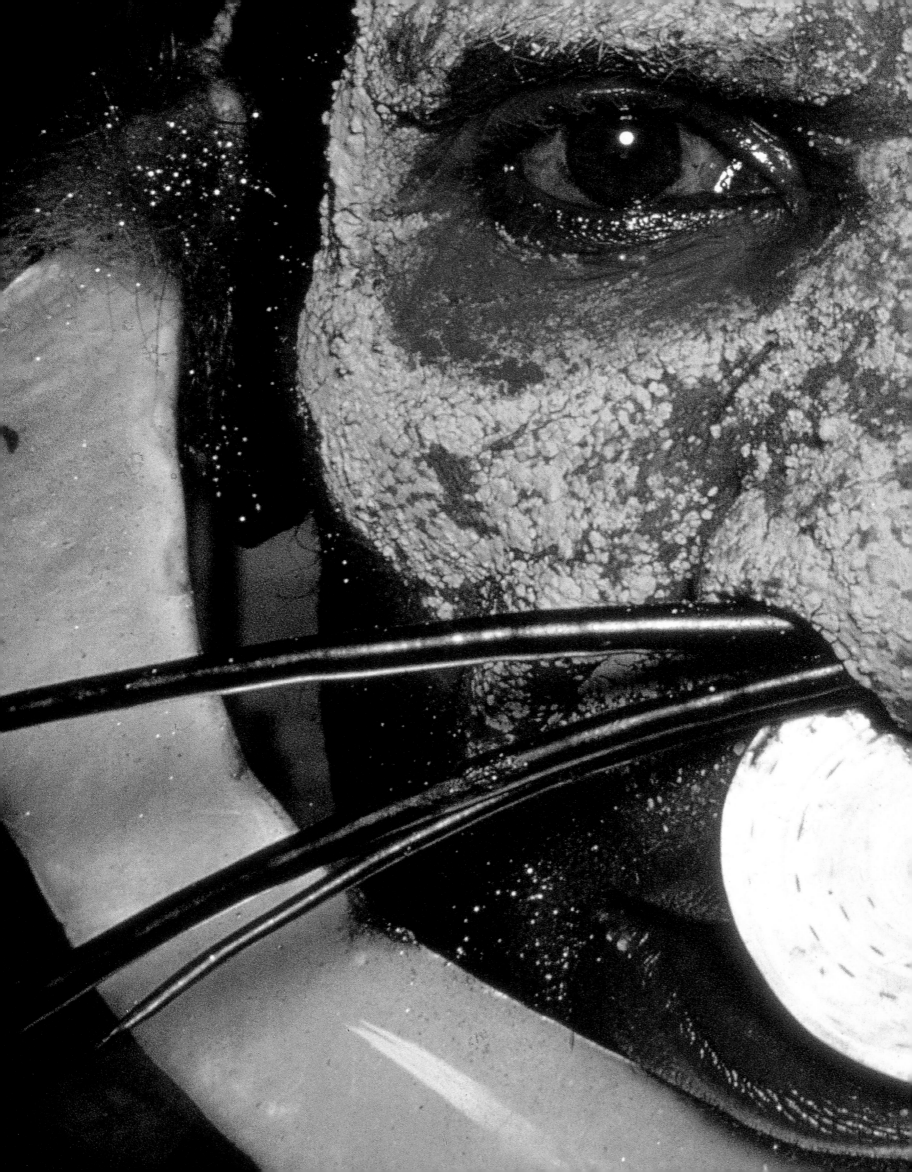

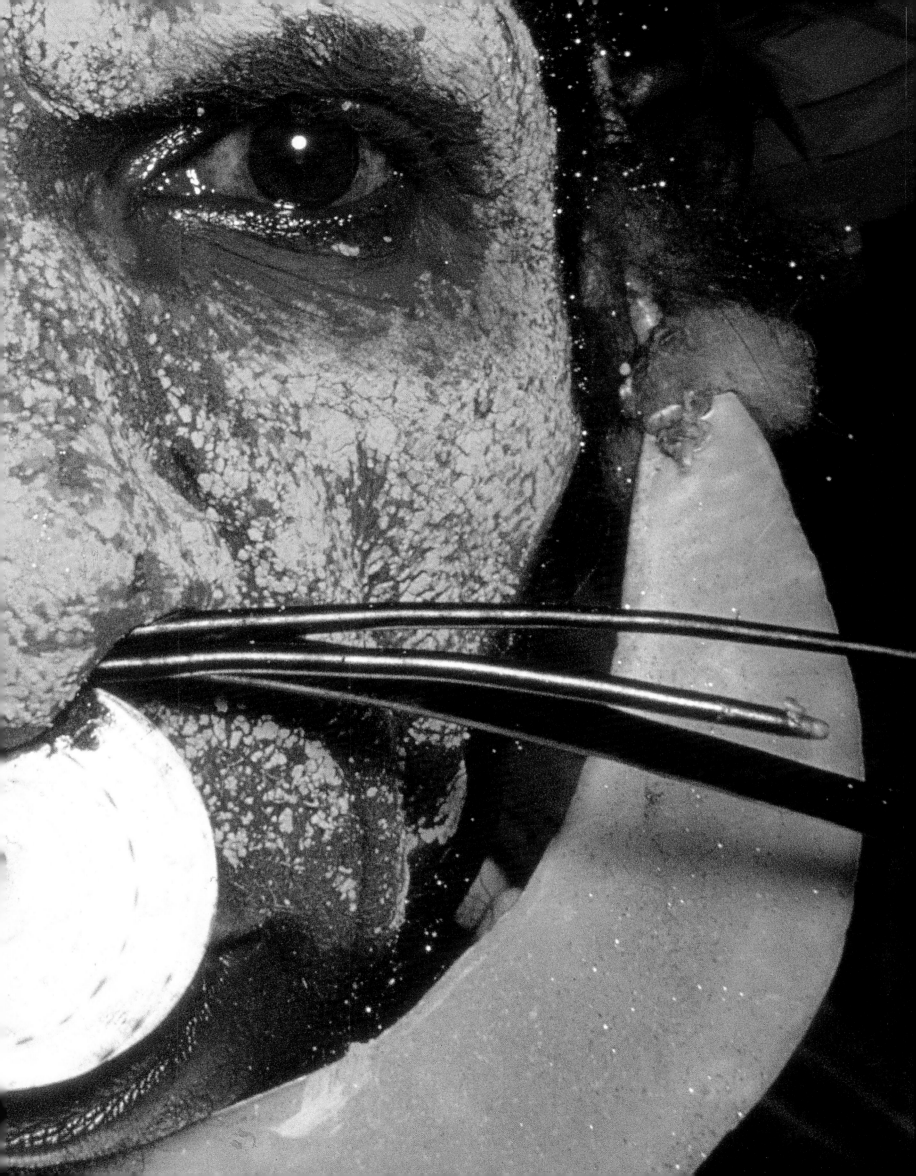

Texts by

Ferdinand Anton
Stefan Eisenhofer
Eberhard Fischer
Ernst Fuchs
Rosel Grassmann
Susanne Haas
Jürgen Lotz
Hanns Peter
Elizabeth Reichel-Dolmatoff
Barbara Rusch
Martin Saller
Reimar Schefold
Heinz Spielmann
Karl Heinz Striedter

Body Decoration

A World Survey of Body Art

Karl Gröning

THE VENDOME PRESS

Published in the USA in 1998 by
The Vendome Press
1370 Avenue of the Americas
New York, NY 10019

Distributed in the USA and Canada by
Rizzoli International Publications through St. Martin's Press
175 Fifth Avenue South, New York, NY 10010

Copyright © 1997 Frederking & Thaler Verlag GmbH,
Munich, Germany
Copyright © 1998 The Vendome Press

Library of Congress Cataloging-in-Publication Data
Gröning, Karl.
    Body decoration : a world survey of body art.
        p.   cm.
    Includes bibliographical references (p.   ) and index.
    ISBN: 0-86565-997-4
    1. Body marking.   2. Body painting.   I. Title.
GT2343.G76   1998
391.6–dc21   98-15366
                                             CIP

Captions to preceding pages
Page 1 Kikuyu dancer from Kenya.
Pages 2/3 Surma painted for a ceremony, Ethiopia.
Pages 4/5 Man from the Chimbu region, Papua-New Guinea.
Pages 6/7 A young Nuba man, southern Sudan.

Preface

Countless thousands of years ago human beings stepped outside their ready-made nature to refashion themselves as works of art in their own world. They became non-natural beings in order to give physical form to a supra-nature that could give expression to their concept of themselves as demons, as spirits and as angels. This has been a characteristic of humanity ever since, continuing into modern times right up to our own day. For me this association of magic and art with visual media is the basis of religion, magic, liturgy, art and the whole world of humankind.

Nearly all these traditions are still alive and active; preserved and nurtured, undergoing numerous changes, they form the thread that runs through dress, fashion and display. Looking at nineteenth-century photographs of Maoris and marvelling at the unrivalled splendour of their tattoos brings home to us what a magnificent and highly individual form of art is lost to us in the West, who have a materialistic view of our bodies.

This self-realization through visual form – a magic path that leads far beyond earthly life into the eternal shape of the individuality of the Human – is an enigma to Europeans. This book lays before us graphic reportage of a fundamental aspect of human creativity and helps us to recognize the uniqueness and incomparability of humankind on this planet.

ERNST FUCHS
Vienna, October 1996

● The loss of an ancient art form. Only two years separate this pair of pictures: the traditionally decorated Nuba man opposite was photographed in 1975; the picture above was taken in 1977.

Contents

Authors

General Editor: Karl Gröning

Ferdinand Anton
Pages 26–67
Dr Stefan Eisenhofer
Pages 112–169
Dr Eberhard Fischer
Pages 188–189
Rosel Grassmann
Pages 230–231
Dr Susanne Haas
Pages 172–185
Jürgen Lotz
Pages 226–229 and 232–247
The late Dr Hanns Peter
Pages 70–83 and 92–109
Barbara Rusch
Pages 186 and 190–193
Martin Saller
Pages 16–17, 20–25, 84–91 and 200–223
Prof. Dr Reimar Schefold
Pages 194–197
Prof. Dr Heinz Spielmann
Pages 224–225
Dr Karl Heinz Striedter
Pages 18–19

Foreword

Elizabeth Reichel-Dolmatoff

Human beings are the only creatures that are able consciously to recognize their own selves and, in the process, their bodies. This gives the skin a special significance, as the final, slender layer that separates the self from the outside world. That is why people of all races use the skin as a surface for artistic expression and embellish themselves with decorations that carry a wide range of different meanings. In this way, through art, they show the inter-relationship between the individual and society and at the same time demonstrate their personal self-awareness and creativity.

A vast range of human experience is thus depicted. The messages conveyed by decorated skin not only distinguish the phases of people's lives, their social and political position and their professional or economic status, they also mark stages in the development of a community. For instance a particular decoration may represent the changing seasons, or it may express mystical, religious and artistic events in the group's life. Through body decoration, concepts of social order and disorder are depicted and legitimized, or specific power and class structures confirmed or concealed. In all cultures body art also expresses the normal and the abnormal, stability and crisis, the sacred and the profane. The decorations vary, depending on the circumstances and occasions (work and leisure, ceremonies, dances, wars) for which they are applied and who is wearing them. The wearer's age, sex and social status play a crucial role. Also significant is who decorates whom, how and why, who is the teacher and who the novice, and whether the process is voluntary or enforced. But people also consciously reveal aspects of their own personality through, for instance, using body art as a way of conforming to their society or rebelling against it.

The form and meaning of body decoration is always the expression of a particular culture. As a result, the patterns used are often found also in other fields: for instance on tools or everyday objects – anywhere that a culture's particular way of life, ideas and philosophy is reflected. The deeper meaning of the decorations can only be understood in this overall context, with changes in the form and content of the body decoration also denoting cultural changes. In this century, for instance – because of the population explosion, the emergence of industrial and post-industrial systems and the introduction of modern science and technology – people no longer decorate their bodies manually, using natural products. They now use objects and methods appropriate to the large and heterogeneous societies of today, with the result that the economic and ideological principles of those societies are reflected in skin-decoration.

Contemporary body art is concerned with highly developed technologies and the complex cultural developments

◄ Tarahumaras, painted for an Easter procession, Mexico.

► Turkana dancers adorned for a festival, northern Kenya.

associated with them. It demonstrates the possibility of altering the body artificially, inside and outside the 'social skin', and shows how the distinctions between man, machine and technology are becoming increasingly blurred. The messages of modern body art are related to modern living conditions, but they are also critical responses to the social and ecological effects of industrialization.

For thousands of years body decoration and body art have been used to express the cultural characteristics of a society. Whether a body decorated in a particular way is seen as desirable, profane, unclean or undesirable depends on the common cultural heritage of a society. Body art is one of the ways in which this heritage is passed on and consolidated, so people react strongly – whether positively or negatively – when they compare their own concepts of body decoration with those of other cultures. This book shows us that decorated skin is a fundamental human phenomenon, and that, despite great differences, the expressive forms of body art – which seek to express, illustrate or challenge patterns of social identification – can help us to understand other cultures. Perhaps this may create a mutual respect, an acceptance of shared humanity and a new understanding of our precarious situation, and so contribute to a renewed dialogue among the peoples of the world. Through the sensitive medium of photography we can find a knowledge and appreciation of decorated skin across all cultures; at the same time these magnificent pictures bring home to us the current state of the human race and of our own lives, as we witness the fearsomely rapid decline of so much of our world's artistic and cultural heritage. We should heed the messages that body art conveys!

● Masai warriors decorate each other with white lime for a ceremonial dance, Tanzania.

In the beginning: the magic of colours

We do not know when primitive humans began to make use of colours and to express their primitive creative impulse by painting their own bodies, but it must surely have been in very early times, in the darkness of the prehistoric period. On every continent people succumbed to the magic of colours and, in their individual ways, followed the primordial urge to embellish and transmute.

They used mineral pigments from the earth, chiefly ochre, which is found in various shades from red to yellow; also the black of pyrolusite (manganese) and the white of lime. Skeletons laid on red ochre and ochre grave goods are found in burials from as far back as the Palaeolithic period, when northern Europe was still covered by ice sheets, and humans were hunters and gatherers. This burial ritual suggests that body-painting was already a long-established practice among the living.

The transfiguring effects of coloured masks and body-painting removed the shamans of animistic religions from everyday life, brought them closer to the divine, and opened the way to new mystical and religious experiences for early humans. The magic of colours and symbols was used for hunting magic, for protection against the elemental, animistic forces of the natural world and for the religious eroticism of the fertility cults, binding humanity, animals and plants into nature's cycles and linking them to the cosmos. Palaeolithic statuettes showing traces of ochre painting, such as the Willendorf Venus, are early examples of the 'power' of colours.

In the sixth or fifth millennia BC Neolithic man made the revolutionary transition from hunting and gathering to agriculture and stock-rearing. Body-painting – whether used to improve the appearance, to identify different kinship groups or for religious rituals – became more refined. Thousands of examples of by now highly developed artistic expression survive from this period all over the world.

When advanced civilizations first emerged on the Nile, in Anatolia and Mesopotamia and in eastern Asia, the make-up used by women of the elite class developed from the 'painted face' used in religious rituals and to denote kinship and status. Egyptian women at the courts of the Pharaohs, middle-class women and high-class courtesans in Athens and Sumerian noblewomen in Mesopotamia anticipated the present-day fashion for make-up, *le maquillage*, by several millennia. Their ointments, tinctures, creams and powders, their mineral colourings and perfumes stand up to any comparison with modern cosmetics.

► The 'White Lady' or 'Horned Goddess' – reconstruction of a rock painting from the 'Round-headed Figures Period' (*c.* 7000–6000 BC), the earliest phase of rock painting in the Sahara. The painting, from the mountainous region of Tassili n'Ajjer in Algeria, shows a dancing woman with dotted body-painting or tattooing, a horned head ornament and fringed arm bands. The culture of this period appears to have been a hunting culture, since no traces have been found of stock-rearing. The picture is in a poor state of preservation, especially the lower part, which has been exposed to strong light.

Rock art in the Sahara

The thousands of ancient rock pictures – engravings and paintings – that have been found in the Sahara testify to the favourable living conditions that existed thousands of years ago in an area that is now just desert. The main centre of rock painting is the mountainous plateau of Tassili n'Ajjer in south-eastern Algeria. The paintings, which have survived thanks to *abris* (rock overhangs) that have protected them from the weather, are mainly in reddish-brown, shading to yellow and white. Ochre, carbonates and kaolin were used as pigments, bound with protein-containing substances such as milk or blood.

The first rock paintings are mainly of human beings, sometimes up to six metres high, and their contents are difficult to fathom. They date to around the eighth or the seventh millennium BC, to the 'Round-headed Figures Period' – so-called from the most notable characteristic of the paintings' style. These pictures do not have the elegance achieved in the subsequent 'Bovidian Period', which began between 6000 and 5000 BC. During the latter period rock painting flourished, with realistic depictions – on a less superhuman scale – of people going about their daily business, as well as innumerable cattle. Stylistic differences and the wealth of detail show that the cattle-herders belonged to various groups and that there were cultural differences between them. The cattle-herding culture declined as the region dried up, and rock painting had a final brief heyday in the 'Horse Period' (from about 1500 BC), with pictures of chariots and horses at full gallop. In the subsequent 'Camel Period' the Saharan rock painting tradition died out.

▲ Rock painting from the 'Bovidian Period' (*c.* 5000–1500 BC), north of Tassili n'Ajjer. It shows a man with body-painting, probably armed with a throwing-stick. Detail from a composition showing men with cattle and sheep and also hunting and butchering an animal.

► Rock picture of a woman with arm ornaments and body-painting or tattoos. This reddish-brown and white picture from the Tassili mountains also dates from the 'Round-headed Figures Period', so called from the circular shape of the heads that sit directly on the torsos. Male and female figures are distinguished only by the primary sexual characteristics.

Painted idols of the Neolithic age

The prehistoric practice of painting the body and face with mineral pigments and vegetable colouring is also reflected in the Neolithic idols, small religious figures and votive gifts. Small stylized sculptures were used in religious practices, but served mainly as prayer offerings or thank-offerings, not unlike the votive offerings in Catholic churches today. They were usually made in an unsophisticated and simple style appropriate to their religious purpose.

The earliest examples of Neolithic ceramics come from Anatolia and the area between the Persian Gulf and the Nile, the great 'cradle of humanity'. The impetus for the development of European ceramic cultures also came from that area in the fifth and fourth millennia BC. Kilns and the new economic activities of agriculture and stock-rearing spread from the Aegean painted ceramic culture to the neighbouring Balkan countries and the steppes of southern Russia. Stylistic elements of the painted Aegean pottery were adopted by the rural 'Starčevo culture' in the Balkans.

Thousands of religious figures have been found in graves and at sacrificial sites in south-east Europe and southern Russia: mainly stylized female figures symbolizing fertility and primitive female deities. In the early Neolithic period they often had huge breasts and corpulent bodies. From 3000 BC onwards, the human figure increasingly became an abstract symbol: a canonical motif used repeatedly for more generalized religious purposes.

◀ Plank idol with incised decoration (*c.* 2100–2000 BC), found in Cyprus. The figure, 27.7 cm high and made of polished red clay, is adorned with stylized necklaces.

▲ Incised image of the third millennium BC from the Cucuteni culture (named after the type site in Romania). The incised carving style was probably brought to the southern Balkans by immigrants from Asia Minor and was commonly used in Transylvania and the Moldau region in particular.

▲ Fertility idol from the fifth millennium BC, found in northern Mesopotamia. The emphatically female clay figure with extraordinarily large breasts is 8.8 cm high and decorated with dark grey and red stripes.

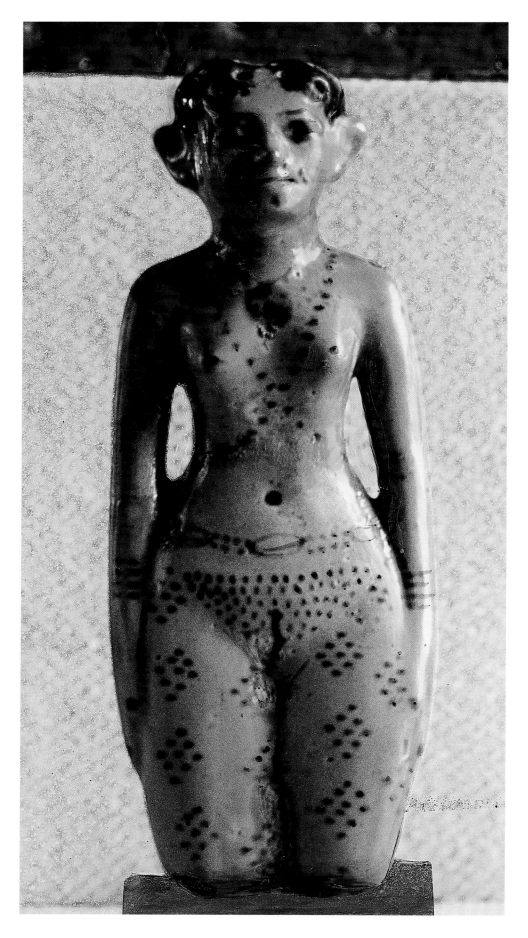

Cosmetic arts under the Pharaohs

Numerous archaeological finds have made it clear that stone palettes were used in the application of cosmetics even in prehistoric times. Under the Pharaohs the cosmetic arts reached a standard of refinement that would seem familiar today. The upper-class Egyptian woman's make-up case was well stocked with powder containers, flasks of tinctures, paintbrushes and flagons of perfume, together with a polished silver or copper mirror.

▲ Greyish-yellow terracotta Egyptian grave figure with incised decoration, *c.* 2000 BC.

◄ In the ancient Egyptian Middle Kingdom (2040–1640 BC) female figures of bright blue faience were made for use as grave goods. The accentuation of the genital area suggests that they were fertility symbols, but they might also have been symbols for concubines. The dotted pattern on this statuette, which is 17 cm high, could be a tattoo.

It was fashionable to have a light complexion, and large amounts of white lead were applied (its harmful effects being unrecognized at the time). Reddish ochre or a touch of carmine were then rubbed into the cheeks to give colour to the lightened face, and the lips were painted with a strong red.

Egyptian women were extremely concerned about skin and health care; they had sun creams, they were familiar with the benefits of egg-white masks to prevent wrinkles, and their eye make-up contained substances to protect them against the eye diseases much feared on the Nile.

Particular attention was given to the eyes, which were accentuated with a fine black line painted around the edges of the eyelids (elbow rests were used for greater precision when using the brush). The eyelids were coloured green with malachite powder; Cleopatra coloured her upper lids dark blue, and her lower lids green. Finally, a heavy black line was drawn through the eyebrows, extending to the temples. The eye make-up customary for thousands of years, and immortalized in countless wall-paintings, gave a distinctive expression to the faces of ancient Egyptian women and men – even the men used powder and make-up.

► The ancient Egyptian pattern of cosmetic eye decoration survived into the Christian era, with slight variations. The illustration shows the mummy mask of a young woman with plaited hair from the first or second century AD. Galenite was used for the short strokes on the eyebrows, and copper hydrosilicate was mixed into eye make-up to guard against infection. Apart from the cosmetic aspect of the make-up, Egyptian paintings also indicate its religious and ritual significance, since washing and making up images of the gods was an important religious act.

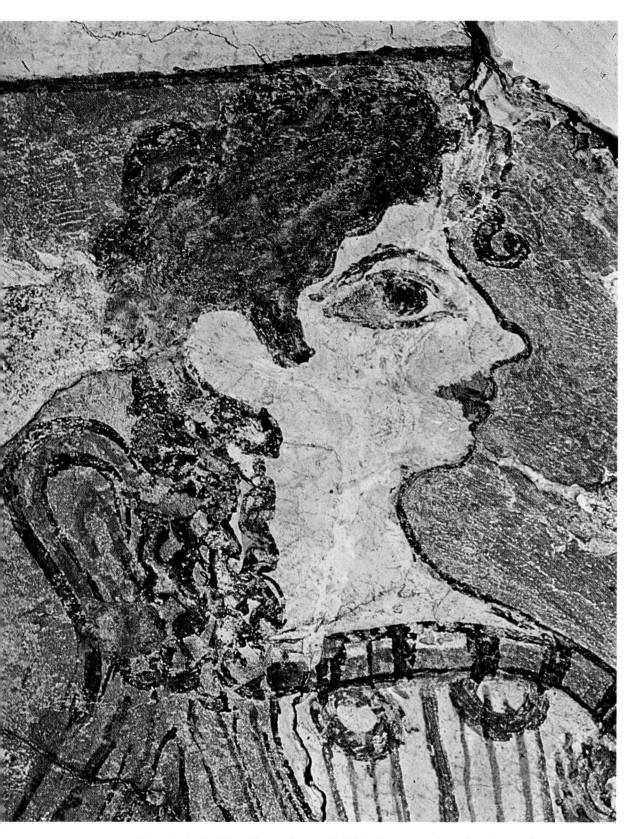

▲ Head of a fashionably made-up girl. This fragment of a palace fresco from Knossos dates from around 1500 BC, the glittering final phase of Minoan culture, which was strongly influenced by Egypt. Knossos was destroyed in about 1400 BC, probably in raids by Achaean princes from mainland Greece, where Mycenae took over and continued the Minoan legacy.

Make-up in Classical times

In Greece during the Classical period (around 500–340 BC) noblewomen and educated courtesans made particularly extravagant use of make-up and creams – especially in Athens, the centre of culture and fashion. White lead – made by dissolving tablets of lead carbonate hydroxide in water – was used as a foundation for cosmetic colours and also to camouflage premature wrinkles. After the face, shoulders and arms had been prepared, the make-up was applied with brushes: lipstick and rouge, eye-shadow and eye-liner. The make-up was removed with soda and ash. Sensuous body decoration was not uncommon. The Roman poet Ovid (43 BC–AD 18), author of the *Ars Amatoria*, paid homage to the naked breasts of Greek women, with their 'rosy buds enhanced with a tincture of gold'.

Sometimes women were so heavily made up that on hot days the whole façade was washed away by sweat. The Attic poet Eubulus (*c.* 360 BC), in his comedy *The Wreath-Sellers*, mocked the fashionable Athenian women: 'If you go out when it is hot, two streams of black make-up flow from your eyebrows, and red stripes run from your cheeks to your neck. The hair hanging down on to the forehead is matted with white lead'

The ancient magic of painted masks survived in the Dionysian cult. At the ecstatic festivals held twice a year for the god of fertility and wine – at which the initiates indulged in revelry and orgies – the actor playing the part of the god and the goats' chorus wore human and animal masks made of canvas. Classical Greek theatre borrowed these masks from the Dionysians, and the great tragedian Aeschylus (525–456 BC) was the first to have them painted in the Severe Style.

▲ Painted terracotta mask from the early part of the first millennium BC – probably a Near Eastern mask used in religious dances. It was from the Near East that the Greeks adopted the Dionysian religion (the oldest theatre in Athens was in the sacred precinct of this fertility god). Both the Greek theatre mask and the close link between the sacred and religious dancing, from which the Greek tragedy evolved, probably have their origins in the east.

▲ Fresco from an Etruscan tomb at Tarquinia near Rome (fifth century BC). Even in the grave, this lady, with her vivid make-up, gives a hint of the gaiety and *joie de vivre* of this sensitive people, whose culture was adopted by their Roman conquerors. The influence of Greek fashion is unmistakable.

◄ Mycenaean female head, dating from 1300 BC. This plaster sculpture shows the cosmetics used by upper-class women of the time. The beauty spots, the sweeping lines around the eyelids and the greatly accentuated eyebrows are a reminder of Mycenae's Minoan legacy and of Egyptian patterns of facial decoration.

▲ Wooden beaker with typical Inca motif. We do not know whether the colours of the face-painting denoted an ethnic group, social rank or priestly function. Inca civilization, southern highlands of Peru, c. AD 1438–1532.

▶ The Aztecs smashed their household goods and put out the fires at the end of a 52-year calendar cycle. In the next cycle the sequence of gods responsible for the days, months, etc. altered. The painting on the clay fragment portrays a god with face-painting and the S-shaped 'speech scroll'. Aztec civilization, Cholula-Puebla style, central Mexican highlands, c. AD 1420–1500.

Ancient America: art for gods, men and spirits

On the American continent, which is thought to have been populated for about the last 40,000 years, humans created an enormous diversity of cultural and social structures, ranging from nomadic hunters and gatherers, through settled agricultural village communities to rigidly hierarchical societies with division of labour and urban centres. The generic name 'Indians' – originating in an error by Columbus, who mistook the continent for India – is misleading because it implies a uniformity amongst the indigenous population that did not and does not exist, either linguistically or culturally.

Long before Columbus, agrarian village communities in northern Central America and western South America evolved into major civilizations that built great cities and temples: the Mayas, Aztecs and Incas. But the process took three thousand years, and it was only in the final phase – in the two centuries before they were destroyed by the Spanish conquerors – that the peak of development represented by these great cultures was reached.

The domestication and cultivation of useful plant species formed the basis of these cultures, making possible surplus food production that was distributed by an elite. It then became possible for those members of society with special skills to be exempted from producing food and become involved in other activities: hydraulic engineers, architects, soldiers, priests and the artists who, through their work, became the chroniclers of these civilizations. Archaeologists have uncovered their creations: splendid textiles in which they buried their dead, painted pottery objects depicting men and spirits and used as grave goods – witnesses to a religion in which the ancestors were worshipped as mediators between the forces of this world and the next.

Archaeological finds show a virtually unbroken tradition of Indian art, including 'decorated skin', over a period of several thousand years. They enable us to plumb the depths of the past and move towards an understanding of the original meaning of the art. The pre-Hispanic evidence shows the highly contrasting modes of thought and expression in the ancient American civilizations. They are mainly visual: thoughts and pictures form an expressive unity in societies that had no scripts, apart from the hieroglyphic and pictographic scripts of the Mayas and Aztecs. Both the archaeological record and the results of ethnological research show that virtually all the inhabitants of Precolombian America painted or tattooed their bodies – for a variety of reasons and in a variety of ways, though not, as a rule, simply to decorate their bare skin.

Body art was chiefly mystical; like other forms of artistic expression it was not random but had a specific purposes closely related to religion or to social and political concepts. It cannot be understood in isolation but must be seen as part of the whole world of native imagination; it was through the colours and the body-painting of the gods or their priests that the spiritual world was organized and expressed. For the Aztecs, for instance, body-painting was 'divine'. It was a medium through which the gods revealed themselves – whereas the office and status of their rulers were linked to secular, non-personal insignia of power: the robe and the 'stool'. The Incas, on the other hand, whose rulers claimed to be the legitimate descendants of the sun god, did not make this distinction. This assertion of the primacy of the sun, consigned the age-old gods of preceding Peruvian cultures to oblivion and initiated a new artistic outlook. These god-kings did not permit images of themselves, so the Inca civilization preferred geometrical patterns.

Fertile women and demanding spirits

Maize (the world's second most important food crop), protein-rich beans and chilli peppers (a major source of vitamin C) were the three main food crops for the Indians. They provided the foundation for the development of a settled and constantly growing population.

There is always something human about gods and spirits, however abstract they may be. These supernatural beings can never completely conceal the nature with which human imagination has endowed them. Male figurines are in the minority in the small village communities of Mesoamerica, with their regular rainy seasons, and the importance attached to female entities in the cult of the dead of early Pre-classic times (around 1200–600 BC) suggests that figurines were fertility idols and points to a matriarchy. For agricultural communities woman was the symbol of fertility; she produced offspring – in other words the labour force.

On the coast of Peru, where only the few river valleys that punctuate the desert are inhabited, the hostile environment created a very different relationship between gods and men. This depended on positive action, the

▲ This clay figure of a woman is an example of the body-painting and tattooing, here represented by red paint and incised decoration, that was already common in early times. Chorrera civilization, central coast of Ecuador, *c.* 800–300 BC (left).

The unknown artist brings out the painting on the skin of the Chinesco lady with a strong red. Nayarit style, north-west Mexico, *c.* 200 BC–AD 300 (right)

▶ Cylindrical or flat stamps, among the oldest industrial products in ancient America, made it possible to print a pattern several times or reproduce it as a continuous strip. The 'pretty ladies' of Tlatilco in the Valley of Mexico – small clay figurines buried with the dead – give a vivid picture of the ideal of beauty at that time and, at the same time, of the importance of body-painting. Preclassic period (*c.* 1200–600 BC).

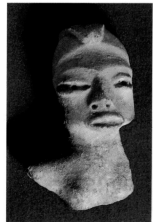

most tangible expression of which was sacrifice. Trophy heads in the hands of priests, warriors and fertility spirits dominate Nazca mythology.

Imperious supernatural beings, mingling the attributes of humans, animals and plants, expressed the exacting demands of the natural world. In this desert region bloody battles between clans or local groups over water rights in the rivers or over fishing grounds and sea-lion-hunting territories provided ample opportunities to obtain other people's heads. The belief that when the head was removed the victim's strength and skills passed to the victor extended to the notion of appeasing supernatural beings with trophy heads to win their favour. In depictions of these deities patterns and colours symbolize their magic forces; the specific symbols included in a warrior's face-paint, on the other hand, indicated the secular standing and rank of their wearer.

▲ ▶ The terracotta vase above shows a vegetation god with geometrical face-painting, a necklace of trophy heads and a severed head as a sacrificial offering. The vessel on the right depicts a priest or shaman, who, from his costume and painting (the stylized bird motif around the eyes), represents a bird god. He holds a trophy head in his hand. Nazca culture, south coast of Peru, *c.* 100 BC–AD 700.

▼ Two trophy heads of woven feathers were used as grave goods in the burial of a chieftain (below). The rigidity of the appliqué eyes, nose, mouth and 'tear-stain motifs' on the cheeks, which are made of gold and silver foil, give these 'dummy heads' a surreal appearance. Nazca culture, south coast of Peru, *c.* 100 BC–700 AD.

Helpful gods, destructive gods

The forms of the Peruvian fertility gods and spirits are localized and at root are based on visual observation of nature. However, in executing individual images the artist had the chance to use his imagination. This scope for variety (which applied to face-painting as well) produced a multiplicity of human- and animal-like other-worldly beings that expressed supernatural forces – one example being a fertility demon with a human body and the head of a jaguar. In Mesoamerica the opposite is true. Here the manner of depicting the gods encapsulates a coherent world of religious thought. The colours used derive from the fundamental concept that everything is associated with the cardinal points of the compass. Tezcatlipoca, the Aztec god of the north, was black; Xipe Totec, the lord

▲ Clay figure of a dancing woman that can be used both as a rattle and as an ocarina. The face-painting motif, a diagonal cross, is similar to the pictogram *olin* (movement), one of the twenty signs of the ancient Mexican calendar, and thus appears to allude to the name: Miss *Olin*, or Mrs Movement. Mexico, central Gulf coast civilization, Classic period, *c.* AD 550–900.

► The body-painting or tattooing depicted on the anthropomorphic vase on the right was probably decorative, rather than symbolic. Huaxtec civilization, northern Gulf coast of Mexico, Post-classic period, *c.* AD 900–1500.

1 This face-painting denotes a dignitary of the Moche culture, northern coast of Peru, *c.* 100 BC–AD 600.

2 In the context of plant domestication, the cross motif on this vegetation god's face may symbolize arable fields.

3 Face-painting from a small figurine of a naked woman that was used as a votive gift.

4 This geometrical pattern (taken from an anthropomorphic vessel) probably denotes the rank of a chief.

5 The protruding tongue symbolizes the demand for a sacrifice. The stylized fish motif around the eyes denotes, or is associated with, a spirit of vegetation.

Illustrations (2) to (5) are drawn from terracottas of the Nazca culture, south coast of Peru, *c.* 100 BC–AD 700.

of the east was red; the god of the south, Huitzilopochtli, was blue and Quetzalcoatl, god of the west, white.

Among the Mayas of southern Mexico the rain god Chac had four helpers, the winds, each with a symbolic colour. The gods' colours also regulated time. Each quarter of an hour corresponded to a point of the compass and its colour. Through their gods humans expressed their concept of a universe consisting of dynamic forces and tensions that both create and destroy. Gods fight one another. In the Dresden Codex (right) the young maize god, holding a vessel that is probably full of seeds, respectfully approaches the god of the underworld and of death. His tense expression suggests a falling out between them. Both wear the face-paint of warriors and are decorated with jade beads. They symbolize the force of the constantly competing deities, which is both destructive and life-giving.

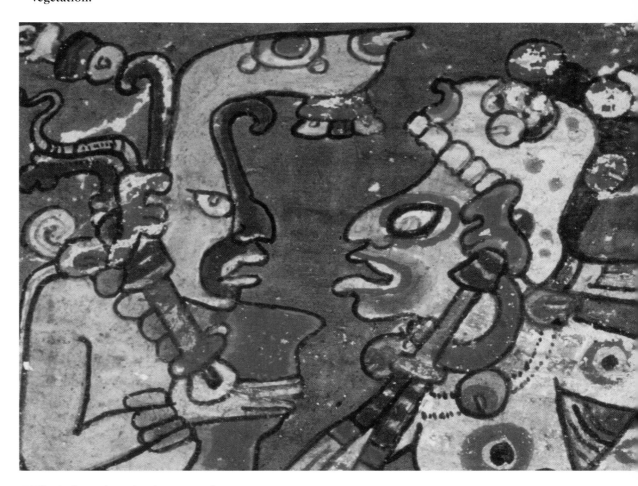

▲ The independent development of a pictographic script in central Mexico and a hieroglyphic system in Yucatán are important achievements. The contents of the Dresden Codex are still largely undeciphered. The fine draughtsmanship and delicately matched colours (made of animal and mineral substances) make these scrolls unique. This example was executed in the style of the Classic period – possibly during the early Post-classic period (AD 900–1250) – after an older manuscript. (Size of detail: 5.3 × 4.3 cm. Believed to be from Mexico or Guatemala.)

Precious textiles and clay idols for the ancestors

That so much of the work of the ancient Peruvians has survived is due to a combination of two circumstances: a favourable climate and religious beliefs that focused on the dead. The central and southern coast of Peru has virtually no rainfall. In addition, the soil has a high nitrate content, which has preserved unaltered the original colours of such fragile objects as featherwork and fabrics.

A fundamental element of religious belief was the lavish cult of the dead and the associated idea of the dead as intermediaries between the living, with their needs, and the forces of the spirit world. The elements of this religion find expression in the textile art of Paracas and in the later painted pottery of the Nazca culture, which give us an insight into the life of these people and their world of profound religious imagination. The textile art of ancient Peru, in particular, is superlative in three respects: it is the most varied in the technical sense (almost all the weaving methods in use today were known), the oldest and also the best preserved.

In the Chancay civilization, which developed about a thousand years later on the central coast of Peru, a certain secularization is noticeable. In the mid-fifteenth century the small 'kingdoms' such as Chincha, Chancay and Chimú were conquered and incorporated into the only empire on the South American continent, that of the Incas.

◄ Hollow terracotta figure in the shape of a naked woman with face and body-painting. Chancay culture, central coast of Peru, *c.* AD 1000–1460.

▲ Two braid trimmings portraying costumed warriors or shamans, wearing face-paint and holding trophy heads. Appliqué embroidery in llama and alpaca wool. Late Paracas/Proto-Nazca civilization, south coast of Peru, *c.* 300–100 BC.

▶ Terracotta figure of a naked woman with body-painting depicting a 'jagged-staff spirit'. The positioning on the figure of the pattern representing this important vegetation god clearly shows the figure's purpose as a prayer for fertility. Late Nazca culture, south coast of Peru, *c.* AD 300–600.

North America: portraits of a great past

On the huge north American continent, between the present day states of Alaska and Florida, a large number of very diverse cultures emerged over the course of history. Their different ways of life were determined by the economic conditions under which they lived, and these also influenced their social and political structures and were reflected in their religious beliefs and rituals. Their body-painting was as diverse as the climatic zones, its meaning and motivation as complex as their civilizations.

As the Spanish, English, French and Dutch settled on the east coast, and later on the Pacific seaboard, many of the Indian peoples moved to the great plains and prairies. The variety of their languages and dialects shows how many small groups existed, even the best known of which numbered less than a few thousand. Hunting buffalo for food became much easier after the Spanish introduced horses into the north of Mexico, and this change, more than any other, marked the starting point of a civilization that, in the form in which we know it, is still less than three hundred years old.

In the early nineteenth century prominent artists such as George Catlin, Karl Bodmer and others went out to the 'Wild West' to secure an authentic picture of the plains and prairie Indians, with their feathered headdresses, warpaint and pipes of peace, their dances and buffalo hunts. It was the life and art of the people depicted by these painters that gave wings to the imaginations of writers and film producers, whose portrayals have shaped the stereotypical picture of the Indian.

The very term 'redskin' is derived from the striking body-painting that was practised in some North American societies and acquired its greatest significance among the prairie Indians. Nowhere else was such importance attached to skin-painting, and in none of the numerous other North American peoples was it so closely bound up with the existence and fate of the culture. In religion skin-painting was of secondary importance, but for the individual it had an important function: it earned him public respect by testifying to his achievements in hunting and in battle. For these peoples – renowned for their warlike spirit, though they had neither officers nor armies – the object of war was glory, honour or revenge, never the taking of land. What they valued most was not the killing but the 'coup': touching the enemy with the hand. Thus a man who could not show any proof of his achievements was seen by both men and women as a coward – a face without decoration as a disgrace.

● (Above) Christoph Weiditz's drawing of these *Indian Nobles* 1529, brought to Spain by the conquistador Hernán Cortés, is 'true to life'. It is the oldest picture of an Indian as seen by a European (above). (Left) The picture of a Cree chief in full war dress, *The Man Who Gives the War Whoop*, was painted three hundred years later in 1848, when he sat for Paul Kane in England.

▲ Wilhelm von Tilenau, a German who accompanied the Russian Admiral von Krusenstern during his circumnavigation of the world, drew these *Californian Indians* dancing at the San José mission in New California in 1806.

'Wild' in the west, 'civilized' in the east

Portraits, like that of the Cree chief on page 34, painted by professional artists, have brought their subjects closer to us, rescuing them from anonymity and making us sympathetic to their fate. But many others who went before them have faded quietly into the past – their faces unrecorded and their existence perceived only in the abstract. To overlook them and their painted skin would be less than fair, and yet few pictures of documentary value have come down to us.

The Spanish settled in California in 1602 and over the next few centuries founded mission stations there. This led to the emergence, on the one hand, of 'mission Indians' and, on the other, of the 'savages', uncompromising groups that were cruelly persecuted and never depicted in western art.

In 1806 von Langsdorf wrote of the small ethnic groups described as 'Californians': 'Many have been converted to Christianity and baptized by Spanish monks . . . These, like the savages, are all passionate lovers of the dance. . . . For the dance they paint themselves with black, red and white; others cover their whole bodies with white feathers; others again paint the clothing of Spanish soldiers straight on to their bodies'.

'Art for art's sake' was unknown to most Indian civilizations. For them art was mainly mythological – although painting the clothing of people from another culture on their skins was surely inspired by curiosity and the desire to imitate. But taking on a Spanish guise had grave consequences for the mission Indians, whose mortality was five times their birth rate. This rendered the missions pointless, but the native culture had been destroyed and, with it, the Indians' ability to survive.

In the east of North America the Indians still lived in a well-ordered world when John White portrayed them in 1585. Skin-decoration served a specific purpose and denoted a person's social status. The forest groups lived in settlements, with agriculture carried out mainly by the women and hunting and fighting the province of the men. The Powhatan were typical. On the coast of what were to become Maryland and Virginia, in a confederation of several Algonquin-speaking groups, a chieftainship with a hierarchical elite emerged under Wahunsunacock. The paramount chief, also known to the whites as Powhatan, ruled over more than 200 villages, which had to pay him tribute. By 1650, however, the Indian cultures of the east coast had been destroyed, crushed between hammer of the English and the anvil of the French.

▲ The people of the south-east attached great importance to decorating their bodies, and experts pricked out whole 'costumes' on their bodies using soot or plant sap applied with a tool made from a fish's jawbone. The English colonists thought that many of the Pomeiok and Pamlico were fully clothed when they met them in 1584. (Right): Pamlico chief; (left): Pomeiok chief's wife with child (left); drawings by John White, 1585.

▲ Strong Wind, Ojibwa (Chippewa) chief, painted by George Catlin 1845.

Colour meanings: symbols of success and victory

The full diversity of the body art of the north American cultures will now never be understood. The meaning of colours varied from one group to another. For most, red was the 'sacred colour' of war: a symbol of success and victory. For Cherokees blue was the symbol of defeat and difficulty, black signified death, and white peace and happiness. But for many groups the opposite was true – white was the colour of death and mourning, and black the colour of joy – so the colour of happiness for some meant the opposite for others. The combination of colour and motif was very important to the individual, who saw it as his 'medicine', his personal tutelary spirit.

George Catlin (1796–1872) was the first painter to take his canvas, brushes and paints to the 'great "Far West"', to portray 'the living manners, customs, and character of an interesting race of people, rapidly passing away from the face of the earth'. Between 1832 and 1839 he visited 48 tribes and painted 320 portraits, as well as 200 oil paintings. He filled several thousand pages with sketches and drawings. Catlin lived with the Indians and identified with them 'as far as possible' and his enthusiasm and patience are reflected particularly in his portraits, for instance that of Strong Wind (left). Catlin's Indian pictures were a complete contrast to the work of his contemporaries, who generally show what are fundamentally only Europeans in exotic costumes. Catlin is equally convincing as artist and ethnological chronicler. It was in his prolific graphic work and written notes that the great aesthetic value and the cultural significance of skin-painting for the prairie Indians first became apparent.

▲ Only the Swiss painter of Indians, Karl Bodmer (1803–1893), equals Catlin in the quality of his work. He painted the two Indians above: a Yanktonai (left) and an Assiniboine (right). Coloured copperplate engraving from: Maximilian Prinz zu Wied: *Reise in das Innere Nord-America in den Jahren 1832 bis 1834.*

► Two famous ball-players, a Choctaw (left) and a Sioux champion (right), were depicted by George Catlin. Catlin explained the game (from which the modern lacrosse is derived) thus: 'the game commenced by the judges throwing up the ball . . . when an instant struggle ensued between the players, who were some six or seven hundred in numbers . . . each time the ball was passed between the stakes [goal] of either party, one was counted for their game . . . and so on until the successful party arrived to 100'. The Choctaw used two sticks to catch and throw the ball, whereas the Sioux used only one.

Ritual dances on the Missouri

Although the various groups of prairie and plains Indians had different beliefs, tolerance and respect for the rights of the individual were essential elements in their religion – and experiencing the world as a whole, in which everything is connected, had the same value and importance. They believed that this world and the next are interconnected, that all natural phenomena (plants, animals, stones, sky, earth, and so on) are informed by supernatural forces with which man can establish contact, and their rituals were based on this belief. Dances, songs, physical objects, decoration and painting were 'medicine': the means to gain the favour of the tutelary spirits. They were perceived by many Indians as the property of a person or a group, things of practical value that were seen as a gift to mankind. For hunting, in particular, 'medicine' was essential, for success depended upon it. Adorned with a bison's head or bear's pelt and imitating the animal's characteristic movements, the dancers sought to achieve a closer empathy with the animal world, so as to make contact with the tutelary spirits. Nevertheless, for reasons of prestige, they made sure that their body-painting identified them as hunters.

▲ (Top). Catlin gives information about Indian dances. Of the Mandan buffalo dance he says: 'this dance always has the desired effect, that it never fails, . . . for it cannot be stopped . . . . These dances have sometimes been continued two and three weeks without stopping an instant, until . . . buffaloes made their appearance'.

(Bottom). 'The Sioux . . . like the fine pleasure of a bear hunt, and also . . . the bear dance . . . one of the chief medicine-men, placed over his body the entire skin of a bear, with a war-eagle's quill on his head . . . and all, with the motions of their hands, closely imitated the movements of that animal'.

► The Chipewa snow-shoe dance was performed 'at the falling of the first snow . . ., when they sing a song of thanksgiving to the great spirit for . . . a return of snow, when they can run on their snow shoes . . . and easily take the game for their food.

The painter as historian and chronicler of a dying nation

It was only for rituals, war parties and special occasions that the Indians dressed in magnificent costumes and painted themselves. An invitation to Washington from President Thomas Jefferson was such an occasion and provided twelve Osage chiefs with the opportunity to dress up in full regalia; it was then that the French painter Charles de Saint Memin saw them.

The complete picture of the cultural background to Indian body-painting and decoration is now lost. The American painter George Catlin does, however, tell us, 'The Osages are one of the tribes who shave the head . . . and they decorate and paint it with great care and some considerable taste. There is a peculiarity in the heads of these people [deformation of the skull] which is very striking to the eye of a traveller; and which I find is produced by artificial means in infancy. . . . This custom, they told me they practised because "it pressed out a bold and manly appearance in front"'.

The great trust that the Indians of Missouri had in Catlin was shown by the fact that the 'head chief of the Blackfoot nation', Buffalo's Back Fat, patiently sat for his portrait in all his finery, with his eagle-feather head-dress, scalp-lock shirt, calumet ('peace pipe') and face-paint.

◀ In Fort Union in 1832 Catlin wrote, 'I have this day been painting the portrait of the head chief of the Blackfoot nation; he is a good-looking and dignified Indian, about fifty years of age and superbly dressed; . . . The name of this dignitary . . . is Stu-mick-o-sucks (the buffalo's back fat) i.e. the "hump" . . . the most delicious part of the buffalo's flesh'.

▲ The French painter Charles de Saint Memin introduced 'physiognomic drawing' into the USA. His watercolour of an Osage warrior (1804) is one of the first portraits of a prairie Indian.

The warrior societies of the prairie Indians

The Swiss artist Karl Bodmer travelled with Maximilian, Prinz zu Wied (1792–1867) on his 'journey to the interior of North America in the years 1832 to 1834' in the upper Missouri area and provided the atlas plates for the account of the journey, published in Germany in 1839.

The prince described the Indians' reaction to the pictures: 'When they saw a lifelike drawing, the Indians said, "Bodmer can write very well", because they have no specific word for drawing'. Bodmer's pictures are invaluable and give a further insight into civilizations already doomed to destruction at the time he painted them.

▲ A Mandan warrior with tomahawk, warpaint and distinguishing marks in the form of feathers and wooden knives as hair ornaments. Coloured steel-engraving after a watercolour (*c*. 1832–4) by Karl Bodmer.

▲ Old Bear, a famous Mandan medicine man. After George Catlin.

Characteristic of the prairie Indians were the warrior societies, of which each tribe had several. 'Dog', 'bear', 'buffalo', 'brave' and 'madmen' societies were common, and membership of some of them was related to age – so an individual could belong to all the societies in the course of his life. Society members or their families had to pay for admission with horses, skins, blankets or rifles. The societies held their dance ceremonies in the communal tribal camps in particular, and each society had its own dances, songs and body-painting characteristics. The Prinz zu Wied observed: 'These warriors in their finery take longer over their toilet than the most elegant Parisian lady. They use fat to rub in the colour with which they paint their bodies'.

▲ Little Wolf, a famous Iowa warrior. After George Catlin.

▲ Massika, a Saki Indian warrior (detail). Coloured copper-engraving after a watercolour by Karl Bodmer also used as an illustration in Maximilian Prinz zu Wied: *Reise in das Innere Nord-America in den Jahren 1832 bis 1834.*

The comparison between the first 'chroniclers', with their pencils and paintbrushes, who came into contact with the people of the eastern forests of what is now the USA in the early eighteenth century and the great Indian painters of the nineteenth century shows the European attitude to foreigners. The two pictures by Charles Bécard de Grandville, drawn around 1700 and coloured later, show 'European' Indians – probably Iroquois – from the Saint Lawrence valley. The oil painting by John Verelst (below left) shows the Mohawk chief, one of the 'four Indian kings', during his visit to London in 1710.

The portrayal of foreigners: illusion and reality in European thought

On the other hand, Catlin in his working sketches, showing Mandan at the solemn *o-kee-pa* ritual, shows a striving for authenticity. These are some of the last items of evidence about the Mandan culture. When George Catlin sought to revisit his Indian friends two decades after his first journey, he found their camps destroyed or abandoned; a smallpox epidemic and the constant battles over now scarce hunting grounds had brought the proud and hospitable Mandan to a tragic end.

▲ The dancer in the middle personifies an animal spirit whose favour the Mandan are seeking; the beaver – sometimes known as 'the little buffalo' – represented food. The dancers on the right and left, whose body-painting symbolizes night and day, evoke memories of a Mandan legend that long ago, when the earth was born, the darkness was driven out by the light.

The affluent society of the north-west coast Indians

The natural environment of the northernmost US state of Washington and the Pacific coast of Canada made the natives of the north-west coast the richest of the Indians, differentiating them in many respects from the inhabitants of the prairies and plains. They amassed possessions in order to show at potlatch festivals how little importance they attached to wealth. The more possessions an individual destroyed or gave away on these occasions, the more he was seen as a man of substance, and the more his prestige was enhanced.

The development of art in this three-class society was encouraged by a highly complex social structure. Elaborate ceremonies served to display wealth and status, and enabled chiefs and nobles to assert their position in society. The ceremonies were awarded to their members by clans, each of which was identified with particular animal ancestors, and had to be sealed with a lavish feast.

At the dance ceremonies masks indicated the tutelary spirits to which the wearers felt bound as well as their membership of the clan, and hence their ancestry; the last factor was particularly important in connection with marriage rules and incest taboos. The 'coat of arms' of his animal ancestors (whale, bear, raven, etc.) was proof of an individual's status, determining his rights and place both in society and in the rituals.

The principles of body-painting extended to the design of masks: the

◄ Technical devices enhanced the effect of Kwakiutl masks. These included hinged sides, movable mouth parts – or, as with this bird mask (second half of the nineteenth century), moveable eyes that the dancer operated by means of strings.

meaning of the abstract markings and
the symbolism of the colours was only
to be understood through spiritual
knowledge. Although the style varied,
this art had a similar function for
all the peoples of the region. The
Kwakiutl loved striking colours and
strong shapes but were not concerned
with detail, whereas the Haida
preferred pastel colours.

▲ ▼ Four painted wooden masks of different origins all demonstrate a strong aesthetic
sense. Left to right: Tlingit shaman mark; Tlingit female mask and Kwakiutl male mask
with asymmetrical painting and moveable eyes. Below: A Haida mask with a highly
stylized bear paw on one cheek. All date from the second half of the nineteenth century.

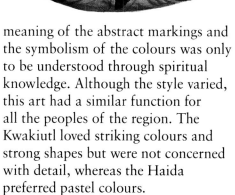

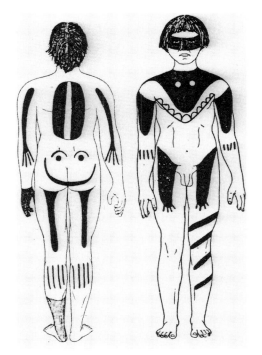

▲ Mask and body-paint form a whole, as
in this example of the Kwakiutl dancer
with painting depicting a bear.

The Anasazi and their tradition

Some 2,000 years ago the Indians in the south-west of what is now the USA were influenced by the Mesoamerican civilizations. They called themselves Anasazi, 'the ancients', although the Spaniards, who came into contact with them in the early sixteenth century called them the Pueblos, after the village settlements in which they lived.

The domestication of maize, beans and other plants enabled this people to make the transition to agriculture. In this low-rainfall area the fertility of the land is of prime concern, and this is the theme of religion and *leitmotiv* of religious rituals – for which the Hopi, in the west, have become particularly famous. The religious costume and body-painting of the dancers is closely related to the fertility rituals, and over three hundred different *kachinas* (goblin-like spirits that mediate between this world and the next) are represented by the dancers, their faces hidden under masks and their bodies painted with symbols. At such ceremonies even female *kachinas* used to be danced only by men, and children were initiated into the world of these supernatural beings with *kachina* dolls. This long tradition is documented in the *kivas*, the underground places of worship, as far back as the Pueblo IV period (1300–1540).

◀ Detail of a Hopi *kachina* doll, Palhik Mana ('butterfly *kachina* girl', or 'girl drinking liquid').

▲ *Kachina* dancer. The helmet symbolizes burgeoning corn cobs. The frog or lizard motif, as a symbol of fertility, was often replaced by hand-prints on the dancer's body.

▶ 'Guabitcani'. This plank-shaped religious figure is characteristic of the Acoma, a Pueblo group on the Rio Grande in what is now New Mexico. The significance of this *kachina* has never been discovered.

Mythical South America

Most South American Indians have recognized the attraction of colours and patterns on the human skin and make use of it with varying degrees of refinement. The inhabitants of the tropical rain forests and savannahs of the Amazon basin were masters of the art. 'To give an idea of how extravagant the naked Indians are with their finery', wrote Alexander von Humboldt in his diary on 9 April 1800, 'I note that a tall man barely earns enough from two weeks' work to obtain enough chica through barter to paint himself red . . . Since the monks cannot sell them canvas or clothing, they trade in red paint . . . So, just as we in temperate countries say of a poor man that he cannot afford to clothe himself, the Orinoco say, "The man is so wretched that he cannot even paint half his body"'.

Large areas of Mexico and northern Central America, the coastal areas of Peru and the areas with navigable rivers were exploited by the European colonists for their raw materials soon as soon as they were discovered, and the increasing pressure of colonization forced the indigenous populations further and further into inaccessible regions. Some groups settled around the headwaters of the Xingú. Their first encounter with white men was in 1884, when they met a German expedition into the interior of central Brazil, led by Karl von den Steinen with an 'acculturated' Bakairi Indian acting as guide, interpreter and intermediary. Now known collectively as 'Xinguanos', these groups had originated in various regions of South America and – after centuries of evasive action, and heavily depleted by disease and genocide – had found their last refuge in the fertile lowland enclave of the Alto Xingú, where the rain forest meets the savannah in the Mato Grosso, and where they live by farming and fishing. Although they have different languages, their culture is relatively uniform, particularly in its religious aspects.

It was a stroke of good fortune that the members of the Brazilian government survey expedition that arrived in the 1940s included the Villas Boas brothers. They stayed at the Rio Xingú in their own mission. Unlike their employers, they saw the solution to the 'Indian problem' not in 'integration' but in protecting the indigenous population. They fought for guaranteed land rights in the region (which has been an Indian reservation since 1961) and protected it against invasion by an alien economic system. Sixteen Indian groups with various origins and languages have settled in the Alto Xingú, an area of about 22,000 square kilometres. With two exceptions they belong to the four main linguistic categories: Ge, Carib, Arawak and Tupí. Between 1970 and 1980 the smallest group had about twenty people, the largest nearly three hundred.

◄ A member of the Waurá on the Upper Xingú with pipe and body-paint. He has probably based the pattern on the spotted coat of a big cat. The red colouring comes from the pith and seeds of the urukú fruit (*bixa orellana*, also known as *achiote*), the black from the sap of the genipa tree (*genipa americana*). The painting has another function apart from its religious significance: the aroma of the painting materials repels insects. (Photograph taken in 1977.)

Festivals: milestones in life

Festivals are mainly communal events. Skin-painting puts the whole person on display, both as an individual and a member of his community. The community agrees the pattern, colour and function of the body-painting and its interpretation, but the execution leaves scope for the individual to show himself as such and to bring his own personality into play. Each person executes the patterns, making use of his individual skills and creating his own compositions and variations – and this individual execution opens out into the realm of art.

The high point of the festive cycle for the Xinguanos is the *kwarup*, celebrated shortly before the start of the rainy season to commemorate the dead and honour the ancestors. This is a depiction and re-enactment of the myth of creation. Wooden posts (*kwarup*) erected in the middle of the village square at the start of the festivities represent the mythical ancestors and the dead, and they are painted and decorated in the same way as the living. Only through the commemorative ceremony can the dead end the spiritual existence that keeps them attached to this world, so that their souls can enter the afterworld. The *kwarup* also marks the ceremonial end of the initiation phase for members of the up-and-coming generation, who in the course of the festivities are ceremonially admitted to the adult community and thus become entitled to paint their bodies in a particular fashion. The cosmic cycle symbolized by death and the live-giving fertility of the new adults is thus completed. Another high point of the celebrations is provided by the *huka-huka* wrestling matches, which help to defuse aggression between the different groups and reinforce the consciousness of a common history.

▼ Two Kayapó men preparing for the *kwarup* ceremony. They have co-operated by painting each other's backs. (Alto Xingú National Park, 1976.)

'Many years ago Maivotsinim went into the forest to chop down trees that represented the figures of man and woman. When night fell, he made a fire under each block of wood, then he sang throughout the night. When the sun came up, the *kwarup* blocks slowly gained strength and, scarcely perceptibly, began to move. And just as Maivotsinim was about to rest from his work, millions of fish jumped out of the river, jaguars came out of the forest, and the two adversaries joined battle. It is said that this was the origin of the common Indians, that is to say those without a family pedigree'. Another myth explains why the wooden posts no longer come alive. Maivotsinim strictly forbade the people to watch him while he was working or to have sexual intercourse that night. One couple disobeyed, and, because of this offence against ritual purity, Maivotsinim was unable to bring the wooden posts to life and so prevent death among humans.

▲ Carefully painted Waurá men with ceremonial decorations preparing for a festival that will start with the *huka-huka* wrestling match (1976). In most villages the houses are arranged around a central square where the men's house is situated, often in the middle. The ceremonies are also held in the square.

Ceremonial decoration and ritual painting: the theatre of fantasy

Women from various communities in the Alto Xingú conjure up legendary matriarchal memories with songs and dancing. *Yamarikuma*, the festival of the women, recalls a myth in which the women fell out with their husbands, the men of the village disappeared for ever, and the women took over their role – and also their body-painting. The mythical episode is re-enacted by reversing the ceremonial attributes: the women don the feather ornaments normally reserved for the men and dance with extra large steps, which is not customary for women.

▲ The body-painting of the Xinguanos comes from intuition and oral tradition. The small groups on the Xingú do not have the educational clay dolls (*litjoko*) that the Karajá used to give their children to help them learn the 'ritual vision' and understand the symbolism and functions of the various patterns. The clay dolls illustrated, which date from between 1925 and 1950, now belong to the past – the area where the Karajá live, a huge river island in the Rio Araguaia, is open to tourists, and the old traditions have died out. Despite subtle differences, comparison of clay artifacts with the painting of young girls shows that the seasonal nomads of the Amazonian rain forest did once have a uniform culture.

◄ Dance ceremonies teach Xikrin children about mythology and religion. (Around 1965)

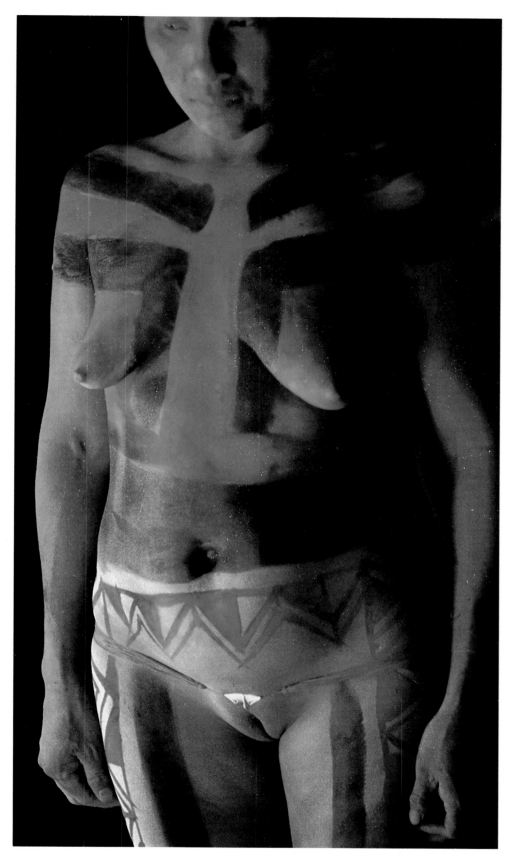

▲ A Mekrangnontire girl from the upper Xingú shows off her costume and jewellery, proud and expectant. Freshwater mussels, snails and the feathers of native species of birds are used for the necklace, bracelets and head ornament. (Both photos 1974)

▲ Women's only garment, the *uluri*, a tiny white triangle of bast, leaves plenty of scope for artistic inventiveness. A Kamaiurá woman (upper Xingú) is decorating herself for the *yamarikuma*. Areas of blue-black, and red triangles, some filled in, some half filled in – all figures and lines not found in nature – form the abstract pattern on her 'costume'.

Filigree costumes made of soft lines, rectangles and stripes

Of all forms of artistic expression, body-painting is the most difficult to define. With its almost unlimited range of variations, it has been the precursor of virtually all the artistic developments that have become familiar to the people of western civilizations only through twentieth-century artists. With incredible audacity, body-painting has combined the most varied of styles – cubism with tachism, abstract act with constructivism and surrealism – juxtaposing them, superimposing them and paying no attention to boundaries or formal moderation. It takes its models from nature: big cats, birds, turtles, fish and so on. The bare skin, with its abstract painting,

◄ ▲ The Txukahamãe from the upper Xingú paint each other's bodies with charcoal and the blue-black sap of the genipa tree. The patterns on their skin are some of the most complex found among the Brazilian Indians. These photos were taken in 1974.

becomes a unifying force for everything that is within and beyond the material world.

For the uninitiated the overlaying of two or more layers of body-paint obscures any clear distinction between motifs and interpretations, but for initiates of the communal knowledge they carry multiple connotations and a deeper meaning.

▲ The most important material for the decorations is intense and durable colour. This woman is applying her ceremonial paint in a thick, concentrated paste.

▲ This Txukahamãe listens carefully ('seeingly') as the *tamai* (a respectful title for grandfather) tells the story of the mythical ancestors. (1977)

With a couple of dots on the face an Indian can slip into the skin of a snake. Brownish-black jaguar spots turn him into a dangerous big cat; with abstract bird's wings on his face he becomes a bird of prey, the king of the air; or stylized fish fins around the eyes make him the master of the rivers. With decorated skin he is capable of almost anything. Only when fighting evil forest and jungle spirits to avert damage to the harvest and fishing does the Indian hide behind a mask. Unprotected, clad in no more than his painted skin, he allies himself with demons and prays for fertility or heals the sick. In the harvest, hunting and fishing rituals that re-enact mythical events in religious cycles memory becomes reality.

Archaeologists revealed the long tradition of this art in America. Missionaries called for body-painting to be banned, when they became aware of the 'magic' on the skins of the 'savages', but ethnologists delayed the process and were able to establish connections and preserve a record of this doomed art through photographs.

◄ A decorated Txikão from the lower Xingú waits attentively for his instructions to be given by the chief. (1977)

Birds' wings on his face make him ruler of the air

▲ This Mehinakú has used charcoal to paint himself with black spots to symbolize the 'spotted jaguar' at a ceremony. The eye motif might be either 'bird's wings' or 'fish fins'.

► Sacred flutes are carved and played by men initiated into mythical knowledge; they must not be seen by women and children. Yakúi – the spirit of their culture and opponent of Añag'u, the barbaric wild forest spirit – speaks through the flute melodies.

Initiation markings

▲ Children undergo initiation rites at the age of about eight to ten, with the ceremonial ear-piercing (*hakatuk*). The face-painting, hairstyle and ear-spools decorated with pearls or feathers denote the various stages in the girls' initiation. Drawings (1) and (2): Kayapó; (3): Txukahamãe.

▼ Kayapó with ceremonial decoration carrying a *borduna*, a type of baton. (Alto Xingú, 1976)

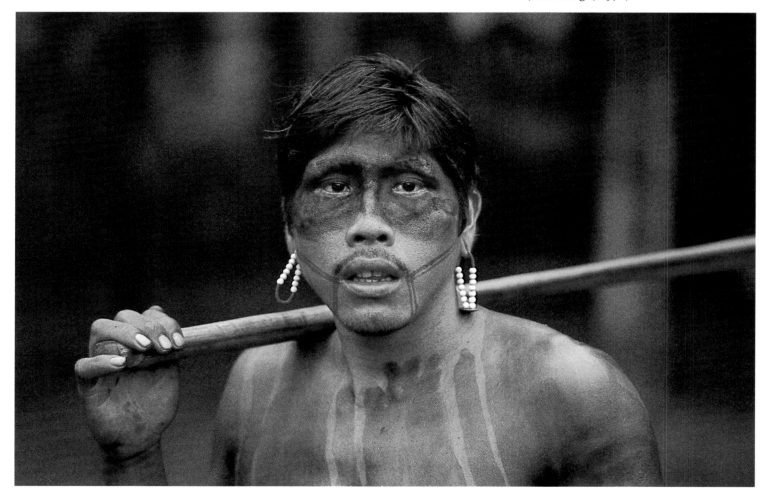

▲ As well as face-painting, the crown of feathers is an essential part of a Kayapó man's costume on festive occasions. (1976)

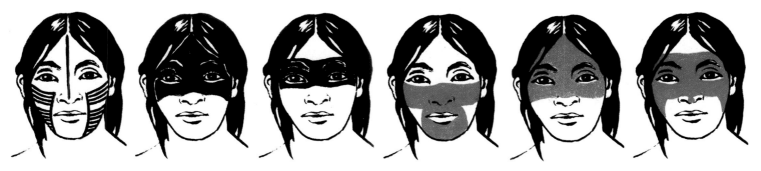

▲ Face and body-painting have to convey a great deal of information. As a result a pictorial form of shorthand has evolved, using a number of abstract marks that anyone not initiated into the mythology cannot understand without explanation.

One source says of face-painting (1): 'The medicine man Cobroti from the Txucahamãe tribe has created the painting which gave him the strength of the jungle snakes for a dance ritual, so that he could get in touch with the dead'.

Little is known about face-paintings (2), (3) and (4) except that they were painted for a *kwarup* festival.

The face-painting of this boy of about twelve (5) is a mark of acknowledgment of the tests of courage that he has undergone in connection with initiation rites. The girl's painting (6) indicates a stage of puberty ending with her first menstruation.

All drawings based on photographs taken between 1972 and 1975.

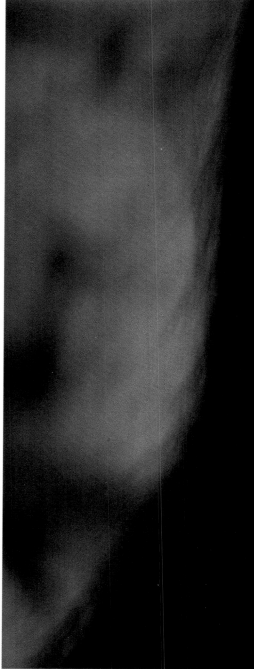

◄ Anthropomorphic vessel, probably for *chicha* (beer, generally made of maize or manioc) drunk on ceremonial occasions. Clay covered with a shiny semi-glaze of resin. Shipibo culture, lower Ucayali, eastern Peru, *c.* 1940–60.

The delicate engraved style of the Indians on the Ucayali in Peru's eastern rain forest

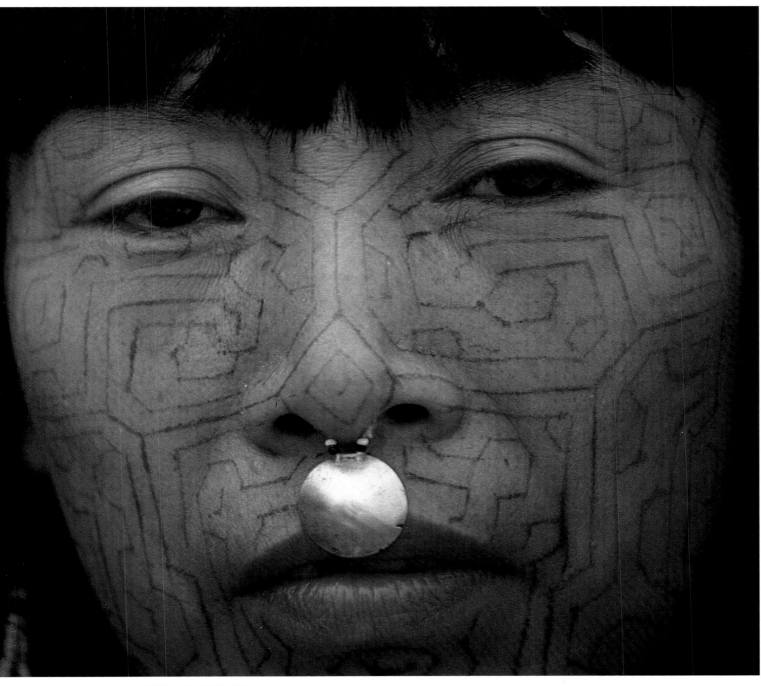

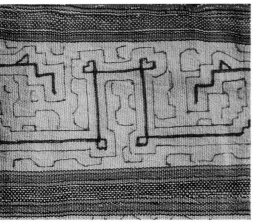

On the Ucayali, one of the headwaters of the Amazon, life is based on slash-and-burn farming (chiefly corn and manioc), hunting and fishing. The aesthetic sensibility of the Shipibo, Canibo and Stetebo, about seven thousand of whom now live in eastern Peru, is characterized by a delicate engraved style. On special religious occasions, after taking hallucinogenic drugs (*ayahuasca*), they read the tunes of songs from this labyrinth of lines. This was explained by the Canibo girl with the round nose ornament, photographed in 1990 (top). A cotton cloth bears a similar pattern (left).

An imperial marriage: prelude to the exploration of the Brazilian interior

▲ Mundurukú with cap and neck flap made from a variety of feathers.

In the retinue of Archduchess Leopoldine, bride of the future emperor Dom Pedro I of Brazil, the Austrian government dispatched scholars, including the zoologist Johann Baptist von Spix and the botanist Carl von Martius. Their expedition to investigate the fauna, flora and peoples of central Brazil lasted three years (1817–1820), and they produced a substantial record of their research, together with an 'atlas', a number of ethnological artifacts and countless drawings. Europeans were horrified by many of the pictures, among them those of the Mundurukú with the trophy head. The cultural background of the trophy-head cult was connected with ceremonies held under the leadership of the most successful head-hunter. His honorary title *dajeboishi*, meaning 'mother of the peccaries', indicates a close relationship between head-hunting and hunting skills.

Like other peoples on the main rivers of the Amazon basin, the Mundurukú (at present numbering about two thousand) were already in contact with Europeans in early colonial times. Today they differ very little in appearance from the rural population in northern Brazil. What happened to the Mundurukú illustrates that today, around the turn of the millennium, photographs taken of the Xinguanos possess a documentary value comparable to that of the early nineteenth-century illustrations published in the Spix and Martius atlas.

▲ Tattooed Mundurukú with trophy head. From Spix and Martius: *Reise in Brasilien in den Jahren 1817–1820.*

▲ Mundurukú with a feather cap and a necklace of peccary teeth.

► These Indian women dancers, corresponding exactly to European preconceptions, illustrate J. Baptiste Debret's *Pittoresque et historique voyage à Brésil* (Paris 1831).

Ancient America · North America · South America

Pueblo is the general designation for various Indian groups that live in the present-day US states of New Mexico, and Arizona. Among these groups, the successors of the *Anasazi*, are the Hopi and the Acoma.

The term *Iroquois* covers a large Indian language family, to which the Cherokee, for example belong. The designation is also used for the the so-called Iroquois League (it actually called itself *Haudenosaunee*) – a coalition of six Indian races of what is now the north-eastern USA – to which the Mohawk, among others belonged.

Sioux covers another large language family that numbered the Assiniboine, Dakota, Iowa, Mandan, Osage and Yanktonai among its members.

North America

1 Acoma
2 Assiniboine
3 Blackfoot
4 Cherokee
5 Choctaw
6 Cree
7 Dakota
8 Haida
9 Hopi
10 Iowa
11 Kwakiutl
12 Mandan
13 Mohawk
14 Ojibwa/Chippewa
15 Osage
16 Pamliko/Pomeiok
17 Powhatan
18 Saki/Sauk
19 Tarahumara
20 Tlingit
21 Yanktonai

Anasazi

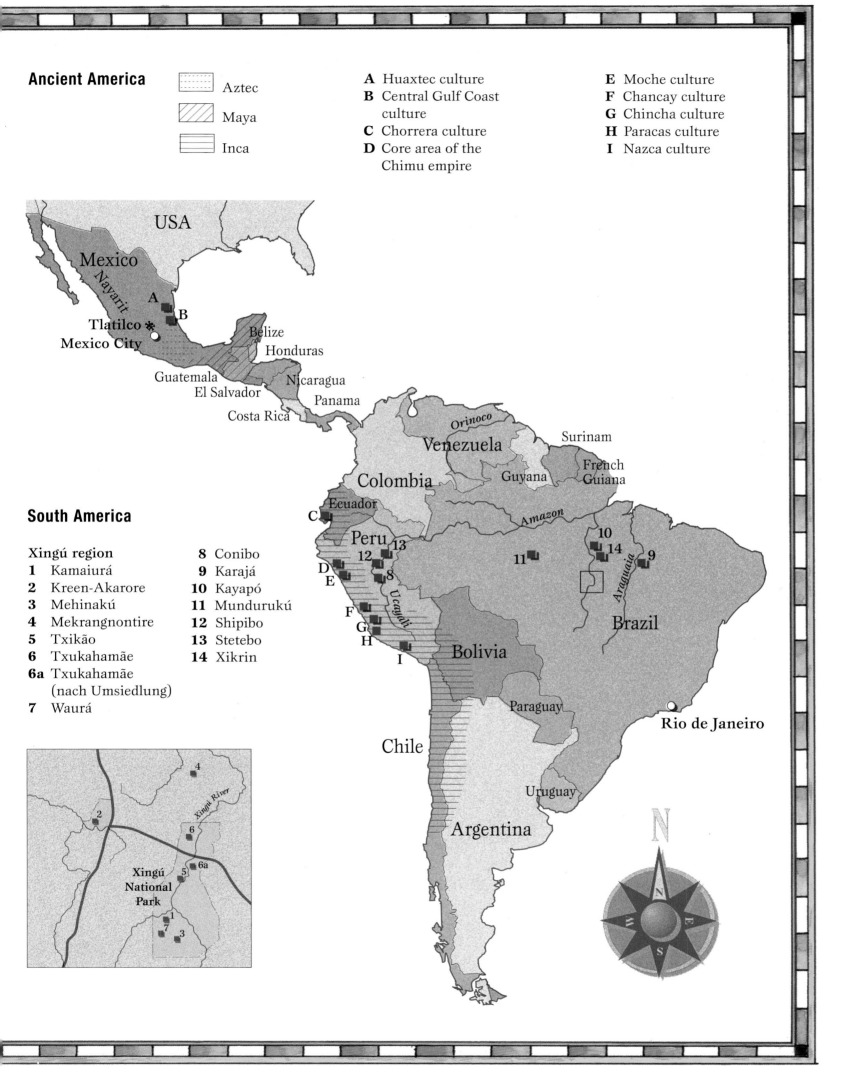

Ancient America

- ⋯⋯⋯ Aztec
- ⫽⫽⫽ Maya
- ═══ Inca

A Huaxtec culture
B Central Gulf Coast culture
C Chorrera culture
D Core area of the Chimu empire
E Moche culture
F Chancay culture
G Chincha culture
H Paracas culture
I Nazca culture

South America

Xingú region
1 Kamaiurá
2 Kreen-Akarore
3 Mehinakú
4 Mekrangnontire
5 Txikão
6 Txukahamãe
6a Txukahamãe (nach Umsiedlung)
7 Waurá

8 Conibo
9 Karajá
10 Kayapó
11 Mundurukú
12 Shipibo
13 Stetebo
14 Xikrin

USA
Mexico
Nayarit
Tlatilco ✳
Mexico City
Belize
Honduras
Guatemala
El Salvador
Nicaragua
Panama
Costa Rica

Orinoco
Venezuela
Surinam
Colombia
Guyana
French Guiana
Ecuador
Amazon
Peru
Araguaia
Ucayali
Brazil
Bolivia
Paraguay
Rio de Janeiro
Chile
Uruguay
Argentina

Xingú River
Xingú National Park

N

The intoxication of colours: the peoples of Oceania

Oceania is the collective name for the 30,000 or so islands in the Pacific between America, the Philippines and Australia. Culturally and geographically they are divided into the regions of Polynesia, Melanesia and Micronesia. The much more poetic-sounding name still commonly used in Europe, the South Sea Islands, goes back to the Spanish seafarer Vasco Nuñez de Balboa, who named this newly 'discovered' ocean Mar del Sur (South Sea) in 1513. When the first reports of the oceanic islands and their inhabitants reached Europe, the name soon came to be associated with the romantic notion of colourfully decorated 'South Sea islanders' living in a blissful state of nature. But the more people learned about the island cultures, the clearer it became that the peoples of Oceania had certainly not found heaven on earth. Where the art of body decoration is concerned, however, the wealth of colours and shapes sometimes actually exceeds the wildest imaginings.

In Oceania there is an impressive range of 'mobile' decorations, the term for the innumerable types of decoration that can be worn on the head, nose, ears, lips, neck, chest, hips, arms and legs or elsewhere on the body. But the 'immobile' decorations are also very important and skilfully executed. These include not only body-painting but also tattooing, which is done mainly in Polynesia (especially the Marquesas Islands, Samoa and New Zealand).

A unique range of decorations occurs particularly in areas where the necessary raw materials are found. One example is New Guinea, part of Melanesia and both the largest and the most populated island in Oceania. With its jungle-covered lowland plains, mountain ranges towering to heights of over 5,000 metres, countless deep valleys and indented coastline it has the most varied landscapes, encouraging the development of diverse cultures. If the smaller neighbouring islands are included, there are nearly a thousand peoples living side by side, speaking just as many languages. Nearly every material that the inhabitants of Oceania turn into decoration is found in New Guinea: coloured feathers of many species of birds (in particular the magnificent plumage of the bird of paradise), snail and mussel shells, colourful flowers, seed pods and a great many more. Particular plants and ochre earths are used as raw materials for paints.

Among some of the peoples of New Guinea face- and body-painting is extraordinarily varied and gives the wearer an imposing appearance, especially when combined with feathers and other decorations. Elaborately dressed dancers, who mostly appear at official celebrations, are an impressive example of colourful magnificence.

◄ A Samo from the west of Papua New Guinea, around 1969, wearing the regalia of the leading dancer at the *hobora* ceremony, at which a recent initiate demonstrates his powers of healing. The variety of materials used is remarkable: the face is framed by a wreath of white cockatoo feathers, with a narrow semi-circle of shell around the chin. The nose-peg is made of a bird's bone, the headdress of dogs' teeth is surmounted by opossum fur and rust-coloured bird of paradise feathers. The necklace is made of cowrie shells, and chains of grey grass seeds hang from his ears. His shoulders and chest are carefully painted with mineral colours to depict a skeleton pattern.

New Guinea: decoration follows strict conventions

In New Guinea the highland dwellers of Papua New Guinea, the eastern half of the island, have developed body-decoration and body-painting into a fine art. As everywhere in Oceania, the purpose of this art is not simply aesthetic. The decorations reflect the social standing of their wearers, which is determined by sex, age and rank, and follow religious precepts, specifically relating to ancestor worship. The colourful painting and elaborate decoration of the men is worn mainly for festive and ceremonial occasions; these can include initiation ceremonies, religious festivals and festivals of the dead, communal hunting expeditions and healing ceremonies, peace-making after a feud and the ritual exchange of gifts between neighbouring groups.

The raw material is powdered charcoal, mixed with water or tree-oils before application. The resulting black colouring is often used to paint the men's faces. Other naturally occurring colours are white (clay, chalk), blue-green and yellow (from mineral earth or plant saps) and rust-tinted clay. Certain ochre clays are packed in leaves and burned to produce a more intense colour. Nowadays synthetic paints are increasingly used instead of the natural colours, because they are brighter than the natural earth pigments; sometimes, however, the two are combined.

● The wigs of these Huli from the southern highlands of Papua New Guinea are made of human hair with powdered ochre added. Like the characteristic face-painting for ceremonial occasions (illustrated here) they pertained to a religion that is no longer practised (*haroli*). The blue and black feathers come from birds of paradise.

Ceremonial decorations indicate wealth and position

In many communities in New Guinea men dominate public life. They lead the rituals, ensure that the ceremonies are conducted according to the traditional rules and pay their costs. Ceremonies are expensive, and before the introduction of banknotes and coins (which have only been in use for a few decades) they used to be paid for mainly with pigs and jewellery. Even today these traditional methods of payment are often used. The men have to devote a great deal of effort to producing the decorations. It is often difficult to obtain the raw materials (feathers, shells, earth pigments, etc.), and many of them are only available through barter. The work is also time-consuming and requires expertise and skill. On some occasions women and girls also wear decorations – provided by their male relatives or husbands.

Wealth is one of the things that earn a man respect and the chance of political influence within his community. However he acquires these not by amassing possessions but by lending valuables to the largest possible number of people or by passing them on in a ritual; this places the recipients under an obligation to him, and so in a sense makes them dependent on him. Some particularly valuable decorative items do not belong to particular people but are regularly exchanged between the men. At formal dances they are worn by the current owner and displayed as evidence of his standing.

▲ Mendi walking through the village of Sangre during a phase of the *mok ink*, 1968. In this spectacular feast pigs are slaughtered and the meat shared out. An adolescent girl from the host clan, *mol shoni*, walks in front. She welcomes the participants and dances directly in front of the rows of men, carrying a digging stick.

◄ Girl from the village of Tente in the Mendi area of the southern highlands of Papua New Guinea, 1973. She is dressed up for the part of the *mol shoni* and will be dancing with the men in an *ink-pomba* ceremony. The red, yellow and blue colours are industrial pigments, the white feathers come from a cockatoo. On her forehead and chest the girl is wearing pieces of shell.

Colour symbolism and patterns of face-painting

Every colour has a particular symbolic meaning, which, like the inherent power ascribed to it, can vary from one Oceanian culture to another. Red, the colour of blood, has a special position and is regarded as especially potent and magical. The Mount Hagen communities in the Papua New Guinea highlands, for instance, believe that the red colouring can help a man become prosperous, and in many parts of Oceania the sick are rubbed with red ochre, which is believed to have medicinal powers. The Mendi, in the southern highlands of Papua New Guinea, interpret certain face patterns like an oracle. They paint a young girl's face part black and part red – the black half symbolizing the spiritual future of her clan, the red the future economic prosperity of her group. If the colours blur during the subsequent dancing, this is seen as a bad omen.

Sometimes individual painting is used to indicate affiliation to a dead person. In ancestor worship in certain parts of Melanesia the facial areas of the skulls of dead ancestors are 'restored' with modelled putty, and in order for the dead to be identified their personal painting designs have to be reproduced exactly on the putty.

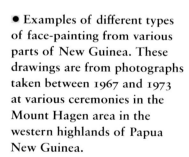

● Examples of different types of face-painting from various parts of New Guinea. These drawings are from photographs taken between 1967 and 1973 at various ceremonies in the Mount Hagen area in the western highlands of Papua New Guinea.

► This 'restored' skull shows the individual painting design of the dead person. The missing lower jaw has been replaced with a prosthesis made of coconut shell. The eyes and hairline are made of shells. Central Sepik, *c.* 1935.

▲ The young Mendi girl is dressed as a bride for the spirits as part of a ritual. The black and red in the face-painting are symbolic, the blackened net bag on her head is typical of a bride. (*c.* 1968)

▶ Ceremonial face-painting of a Mendi. The face is blackened with powdered charcoal, and the nose and mouth accentuated with bright artificial colours. White clay emphasizes the eyes and beard. Mendi area, village of Tente, southern highlands of Papua New Guinea, 1970.

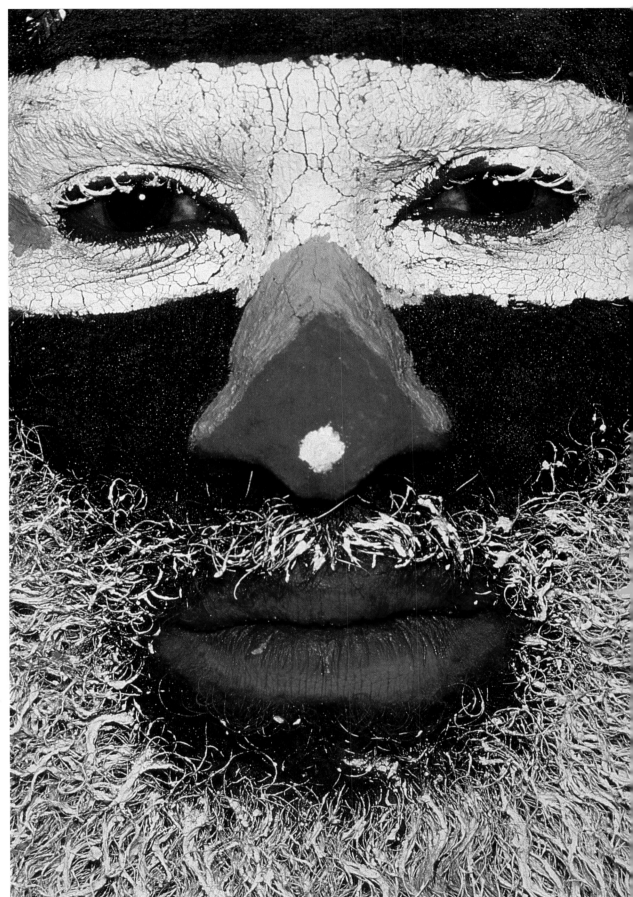

1|

2|

3|

4|

5|

Decoration and paint: sacred power for men and plants

The Maprik area is a centre of the yam cult in Papua New Guinea. The yam roots, almost four metres long and weighing two hundredweight, are grown for the cult in special gardens. They are cultivated intensively by covering them with a red colouring matter that is believed to have special properties. The decorated roots are ritually exchanged between the men of the group at the climax of the ceremony. The men dress up especially carefully for the yam and ancestor-worshipping ceremonies. Particular attention is paid to the head, as the centre of vitality and spiritual strength. The decorations have deep symbolic significance; some – particularly birds' feathers, dogs' canine teeth and boars' tusks – are believed to have sacred powers. Through the decoration and painting the men express their relationship with supernatural powers and come closer to the essence of deified ancestors.

1 Upper part of a cult statue from the Maprik area.
2 A wickerwork house mask from the village of Tunggimbit, Blackwater River, Papua New Guinea.
3 Head of a cult statue from the Maprik area. The use of yellow and red ochre to paint figures is characteristic of this area.
4 Upper part of an ancestor figure from the central Sepik area, painted with mineral colours.
5 Figure-shaped upper part of a ceremonial chair from the central Sepik area of Papua New Guinea. Ceremonial chairs are amongst a clan's most sacred objects. They are not for sitting on but are used as a kind of lectern.

▶ Head of one of the over-lifesize ancestor figures erected in places of worship in the Maprik area. They play an important part in the yam cult.

▲ Dancer from the Fly River area in ceremonial costume. From an art supplement, *c.* 1925.

◄ This *tago* spirit mask made of bast (*tapa*) is stretched over a light frame. The festivals associated with this religion are held only once every ten to twelve years and last for a whole year. Huon Gulf Tami (eastern New Guinea).

Unmistakable ornaments: symbols of higher beings

In many parts of Melanesia objects of worship are kept in their own building (the house of worship, house of the spirits or men's house), the whole of which is sometimes seen as a creator being, as indicated by the huge gable masks attached to the outside of the building above the main entrance. Many of the masks and ritual figures are decorated with artful paintings and ornamental carving in the tribe's customary face- or body-painting patterns, for they are perceived as creator beings – clan forebears or dead ancestors – who are identified by their ornamentation. It is believed that only when the painting is finished will the carving be filled with the power of the cultural heroes or ancestors.

In many areas material from the bast (inner bark) of the paper mulberry is used for the masks. The artist stretches this material, known as *tapa*, over a wickerwork frame and shapes it into a mask to be worn over the head or face. The mask is then painted as desired, by either attaching coloured pieces of *tapa* or applying paint. The bast masks worn by the inhabitants of the Tami area of Papua New Guinea represent clan spirits, recognizable by their own unique decorations.

The inhabitants of the Sepik area, too, are unable to vary the decorations on their masks at will. The patterns have to correspond exactly to the pattern that the dead person wore when alive – to which he had an exclusive right, and which no one could copy. Spirits and demons also have their distinctive individual decorations.

● Examples of how mask painting reflects the individual facial patterns of the clan forefathers or dead ancestors. Top: mask from the Sepik area, north-eastern New Guinea. Bottom: lower half of a mask representing the sago-bringer Moem. The face is modelled from clay and resin over the skull, then painted and finished with snail shells and human hair. East Iatmul, Kararao, central Sepik.

Protective clay: symbol of mourning and death

It is common practice in Oceania to cover the face, head or even the whole body with clay as a sign of mourning after the death of a close relative. Painting is in many cases intended as concealment from the dead person's spirit, widely believed to represent a major threat to the living. Only after a lavish ceremony, in which the spirit of the dead person is symbolically led to the next world by decorated mask wearers, is the threat of danger banished, and the mourning costume can be removed.

In some areas clay also plays a part in boys' initiation ceremonies. For instance a layer of clay is applied to the wounds of newly circumcised novices, clay being believed to have magic powers to heal the wound more quickly. Sometimes the whole body of the initiate is covered with clay, in the same way as for mourning; this is connected with the idea that the boy 'dies' during the initiation and is reborn as a mature adult.

The clay masks of the inhabitants of the Asaro valley developed by chance, according to their account. Once, when their village was attacked and they were outnumbered, the warriors fled and hid in the mud on the bank of the Asaro river. After some time they sent out scouts to see whether the enemy had retreated, but while the scouts were creeping cautiously back to the village, the river mud dried on their bodies. Seeing these clay-encrusted figures, the enemy mistook them for evil spirits and took flight. The Asaro valley inhabitants hold ceremonies to commemorate this incident, at which the dancers cover their bodies with clay and put clay masks over their heads.

◄ A man from Chuave in the Chimbu area. Bamboo horns are set into his clay helmet, and his fingers are accentuated by sharpened bamboo canes. The necklace is made of pigs' teeth and empty seed-cases. He is probably imitating the 'mud men' of the Asaro river.

▲ A 'mud man' from the Asaro river region in the eastern highlands, covered from head to foot with clay. As the clay cracks and peels off, it may symbolize the flesh of a decomposing body.

▲ Nineteenth-century helmet mask from the Vitu Islands, New Britain, probably representing an important ancestor with his special face-painting.

▲ Sulka wickerwork mask. Woven out of flexible reeds, with red-painted pith strips sewn on. Gazelle peninsula, south-eastern New Britain.

▲ Baining *tapa* mask. The red-and-black-painted bark bast is stretched across a framework of bent sticks. The dancer wearing the mask can only see through the mouth opening. The eyes are marked with concentric circles in imitation of the patterns of the remodelled ancestors' faces. Gazelle peninsula, south-eastern New Britain, 1911.

New Britain: island of masks

In New Britain impressive forms of Melanesian mask art have evolved: wonderful creations of woven fibres and plants, stretched over a cane framework and painted. Many of these expressive works of art have been created for the members of secret societies who, in their rituals, often attach decorations made of fibres, bark and leaves to the face-masks and decorate their bodies in the same way. The best-known secret societies are the *duk-duk* and, among the Tolai – who have migrated to the neighbouring island of New Ireland – the *iniet*. *Duk-duk* members wear conical black fibre masks with a crest on top; at their initiation *iniet* novices are given small magic figures carved out of limestone. The Baining (related to the Papua), who have been driven into the mountainous hinterland, have the most fantastic and impressive masks of all. The best known are huge constructions – up to twelve metres (40 ft) high – made of plaited fibre; supported by a number of bearers with bamboo poles, these are used at ancestor ceremonies and then destroyed. For the impressive Sulka masks tough, porous strips of pith from a type of reed are applied over a base made of plaited reeds, and facial features (nose, etc.) made from pieces of wood are then attached. Again these masks are only used once. They are painted dark red, with the secret society and ritual symbols added in black, white, blue and green. Typically, they are topped with pointed caps – which are also used for double masks – and incorporate blue and green colouring derived from plant saps found only in New Britain.

▶ **Siassi dance mask. The concentric circles around the eyes are similar to those on the Baining ancestor faces. Western New Britain, 1940.**

New Ireland: *malanggan* symbols

The most extraordinary, varied and formally perfect Melanesian art forms developed on the island of New Ireland in the Bismarck archipelago. A wealth of figures, masks, stylized animals and fabulous beings has been preserved. On bas-reliefs and ancestor memorials, humans and animals are woven into arabesques of subsidiary figures and ornaments that carry a profound symbolism. The varied carvings are known as *malanggan*, after the ceremonial cycles (*malanggan*) that form the religious high points of the inhabitants' lives. Created by wood-carvers working in

▲ This head, painted with natural colours, is part of a *malanggan*, an ancestor memorial, whose powers were believed to protect village communities and families. (1932)

◄ Tatanua dance mask of painted wood, worn in *malanggan* ceremonies. Each family group has its own particular mask decoration.

seclusion and according to fixed rules, the *malanggan* are displayed at major ceremonies for the dead and the ancestors, at rituals invoking the tutelary spirits and at initiation ceremonies for the young men and women. *Tatanua* masks, with piled-up bast-fibre coiffures modelled on mourning hairstyles, are worn at ritual dances. Also characteristic of New Ireland art are *uli* figures: wooden statues carved in one piece, which are ritually painted and displayed at a series of ceremonies spread over three years.

▲ A fanciful symbol of the monthly changes in the moon. The woman of the dark moon is sinking into a fish-head. This painted wooden figure for a boat ornament was displayed at ancestor ceremonies. (*c.* 1880)

▶ An *uli* from the north part of the island. This cult figure symbolizes a higher being. The head is always painted with warpaint, and its helmet-like structure symbolizes the mourning hairstyle worn after a war party.

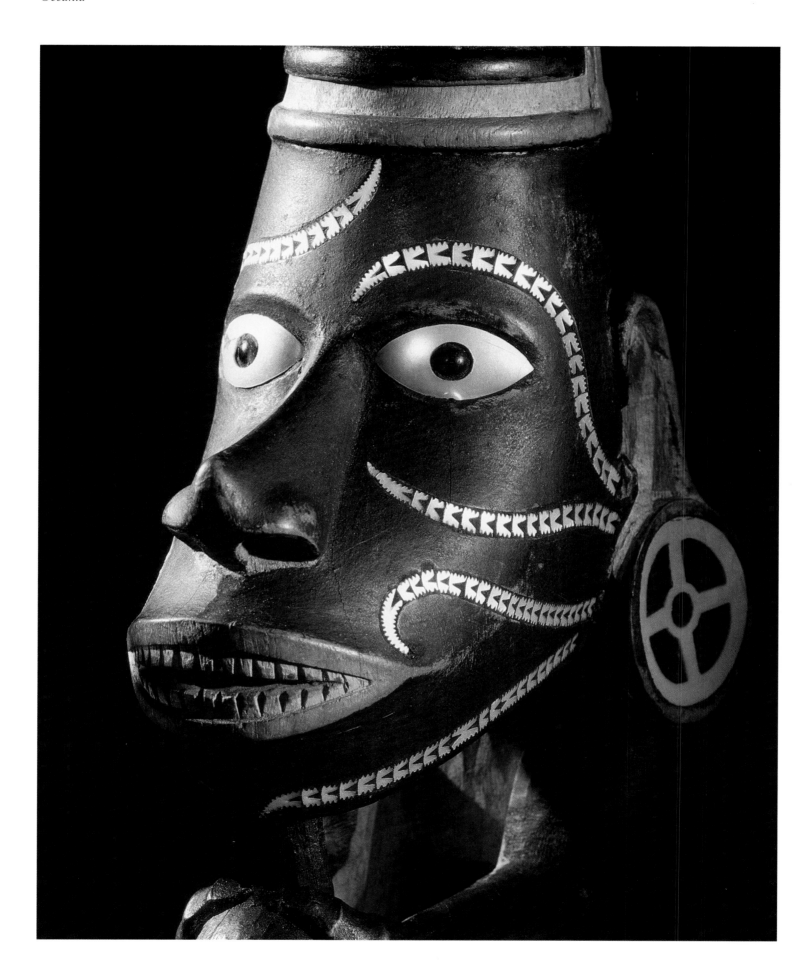

Tattooing and inlaid work: art on the Solomons

When the Spaniard Alvaro de Mendaña 'discovered' the Solomons in 1568, he was searching for the legendary Ophir, which the Bible mentions as the source of the gold for King Solomon's temple. This hope was frustrated, but the archipelago was still named after King Solomon.

Typical of the Solomonese wood-carver's art are the figureheads on plank boats, representing the tutelary spirit of fishermen and head-hunters; the muzzle-like mouth is reminiscent of the mythological dog who once taught men their culture. The religion is based on ancestor-worship, and people believe that the spirits of the dead are always present. Dead chiefs remain in the community; their skulls, 'restored' by modelling, are preserved and worshipped. The head is believed to be the seat of supernatural powers, and this explains the head-hunting that used to be customary – the power passes to the warrior who kills the enemy and takes the skull.

▲ This small limestone head decorated with tattoos represents a *tindalo*, a kind of spirit. A *tindalo* can live in a bush, a pool or even a rock. Southern part of Choiseul island, nineteenth or twentieth century.

◄ Part of a prow figure (*c.* 1850). The nautilus-shell inlay panels, which are typical of the south Solomons, probably represent the tattoos of the dead.

▲ Prow figure with shiny turtle-shell inlay from New Georgia, Solomon Islands. The mouth, similar to a dog's muzzle, is particularly prominent on this figure.

▲ Painted mask made of tree-fern wood, from the south of Malekula.

◄ The traditional painting on the face of this young Namba woman (1970) is similar to that on the small mask made of light vegetable materials with banana trunk fibre decoration, illustrated above it, which came from the island of Aoba at around the turn of the century.

Vanuatu: painting shows who you are

Secret societies for men and women exist in many communities on Vanuatu (formerly the New Hebrides). The men's societies, in particular, used to have a strong influence on social and political life. These are hierarchical communities in which men acquire membership at the various levels by gifts of pigs. Each rank has its own rights and duties, among them the right to wear the appropriate form of face-painting and body decoration at ceremonies and dances.

In some groups, such as the Namba on Malekula, a traditional burial ritual is still practised. The body is laid on a wooden grille in the house of the dead, covered with leaves and left for a long time until it becomes a skeleton. For the wake the skull is 'remodelled' to represent the facial features and painting of the deceased as accurately as possible and attached to a body made of vegetable materials (the actual body is buried). After several days of festivities to celebrate the deceased, at which ritual dances are performed and pigs eaten, the modelled skull is kept in the men's house and its plant body is thrown away.

► Cult figure from the island of Malekula. The head is carved from tree-fern roots, and the limbs are made of rolled dried banana leaves covered with a vegetable paste. The lower face, painted in solid blocks of colour, represents the cannibal woman Nevimbumbaau; above her is her husband or son. Homage was paid to them at the harvest festivals in a Seniang village in the south of the island.

Masters of the tattooist's art: the Polynesians

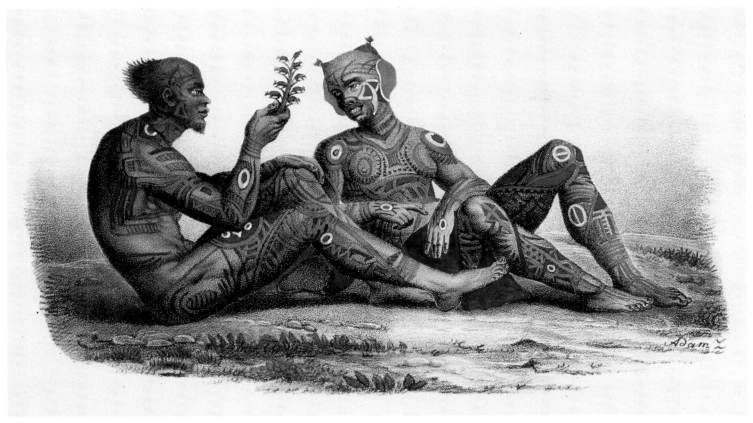

▲ Men from the Marquesas Islands, nineteenth century. Their tattoo patterns explain why the Europeans thought at first that they were wearing lace-decorated clothing.

The English word 'tattoo' comes from the Tahitian root *tatau* ('to inflict wounds'). The decoration of the body with tattooed patterns is common in many parts of Oceania, but the inhabitants of the Marquesas Islands in eastern Polynesia have developed it into a fine art. The Spanish seafarer Alvaro de Mendaña, the first European to put into these islands in 1595, mentioned the artistic decorations that covered the entire bodies of the islanders.

Tattooing involve making patterns in the skin with a needle or an adze-

◄ Elaborately decorated warrior from the Marquesas Islands, nineteenth century. The chessboard tattoo pattern that used to be common went out of fashion in the mid-nineteenth century for no apparent reason.

shaped implement (the 'tattooing comb') dipped in colouring matter, which penetrates the subcutaneous tissue and colours it permanently. For the colouring matter the Polynesians used an oily soot, obtained by burning seeds and mixing it to a fine paste with coconut oil. This pricking or colour tattooing is very different from scarification – which in Oceania is mainly confined to the Melanesian islands – in which the skin is incised or burnt to form the patterns.

Generally speaking women in Polynesia were less heavily tattooed than the men. On the Marquesas Islands, for instance, men from noble families had patterns all over their bodies, whereas the women usually only had decorated faces and limbs. Polynesian boys normally had their first tattoos between the ages of

twelve and eighteen. The exact time depended on when the chief's son was first tattooed, for all the boys of the same age in his district were tattooed with him. Girls were first tattooed when they became sexually mature.

Only small areas of skin were tattooed at any one time; the process was then resumed days or weeks later. It often took decades to decorate the whole body.

Marks of prestige, mourning and obligation

▲ According to traditional rules of art, every master tattooist has his own sequence for applying patterns on the different parts of the body. These decorations, which are partly prepared beforehand on templates, may vary in composition but are made up of recurring individual elements, each of which has its own name. The name refers either to the (sometimes highly stylized) object to be depicted or to the particular part of the body on which it is applied. (Samoa, 1973)

According to Polynesian mythology, humans learned tattooing from the gods. Such decoration was therefore applied in a ritual and ceremonial context by particularly revered masters.

The costly patterns were a visible sign of prosperity and conferred prestige. They increased a person's chances of finding a partner and his prospects of success in battle. To heap further disgrace on dead enemies, they were ritually eaten – and in the Marquesas Islands this was only permitted to those who were tattooed. The Hawaiians had their tongues tattooed as a sign of mourning, whilst on Rorotonga mourning patterns were tattooed on the neck and chest. Men on the Marquesas Islands who had to pursue a blood feud were marked on their cheeks, their wives on their chests and shoulders.

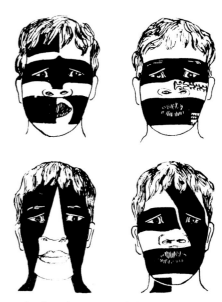

▲ The facial tattoos of the Marquesas islanders consisted mainly of dark areas. The particular way in which they were arranged identified the wearer. Bast casings for skull remains were painted in the same way.

▲ On the Marquesas Islands members of the upper class – both men and women – also had the backs of their hands tattooed. Although individual motifs recur frequently, no two patterns are the same.

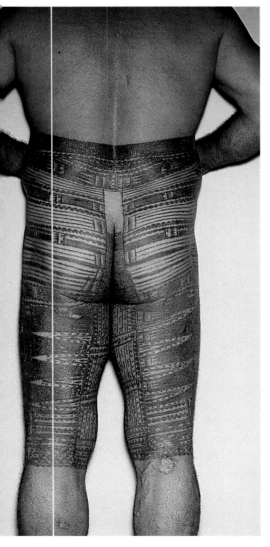

▲ Example of a tattoo pattern on thighs and buttocks of Samoan man. (1975)

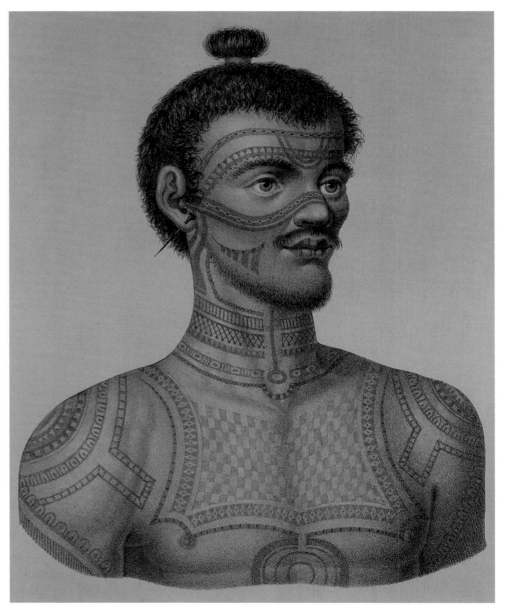

▲ Head and shoulders of a tattooed man on Nuva-Hiva, the largest of the Marquesas Islands, c. 1920. With growing European influence, foreign elements increasingly adulterated the traditional patterns. Instead of the decorations that had been handed down, written characters copied or animals depicted. Sometimes an attempt was even made to imitate European clothing in the tattoo patterns.

Moko: decoration, sign of rank and coat of arms

Moko is the name that the Maoris of New Zealand give to their particular tattoo pattern; its basic and most important element is the spiral. The Maoris used it to create intricate and unique artistic designs.

In the hierarchical society of the Maoris, tattooing was a prerogative of the noble and free. Priests simply wore a small pattern above the right eye as a symbol of their rank, whilst slaves were forbidden to have any form of tattoo. Women had far fewer tattoos than men. Body-tattooing was also common among the Maoris, but facial decoration was considered more important; the unique *moko* tattooed on a man's face was a symbol of his identity – indeed it was his coat of arms. Such *mokos* could be copied, line by line, and in early contacts with Europeans were used as signatures.

In the nineteenth century the Maoris put up a strong resistance to the English invasion, but even in pre-colonial times battles were not uncommon. Victors cut off the heads of conquered enemy chiefs and put them on the palisade surrounding their village; the heads of their own leaders were preserved and venerated. A peace agreement was unthinkable without a mutual exchange of the heads that had been taken. However, the preserved heads coveted in the nineteenth century by European sailors rarely came from chiefs; the Maoris tattooed the bodies of slain enemies, prisoners of war or slaves, and later treated their skulls and sold them for a high price.

◄ This painting by Gottfried Lindauer shows Tamati Waka Nene, an important Maori chief in the early nineteenth century, with a decorated club. In close combat the Maoris mainly used sticks or flat clubs.

▲ Artistically carved mask from a house gable, nineteenth century.

▶ Tauhiao, Maori chief, *c.* 1880.

▲ Tattooed Maori, *c.* 1890.

▶ Portrait of a chief with a narrow wooden comb and a facial pattern of curved lines, 1773. From a drawing by Sydney Parkinson, who accompanied Captain Cook on his first expedition.

Lines carved on the skin

▲ Detail of a carving on a house, 1842. The carving – a self portrait of Raharuhi Rukopo, master carver of the house of Te Hau ki Turanga – was made in Manutuke, near Gisborne. Rukopo apparently owned a complete set of European carving tools, which he used to develop new styles. The metal tools gave greater creative freedom than the traditional tools made of stone.

Maori tattooing is unusual, because of the method used. In many parts of Oceania needle combs were used to tattoo the body, but the spiral lines of Maori face-tattoos were usually made with chisel-like implements working directly on the outer surface of the skin.

Like Maori carving, tattoos were carried out by revered and highly paid experts, *tohunga-ta-moko*. The first tattoo was applied after puberty, but it often took several years before the pattern was complete, since the painful process could only be carried out in a number of separate stages. With a few exceptions, women were forbidden to tattoo their foreheads and chins, but, since a red mouth was considered ugly, the lips were tattooed to give them a blueish appearance.

For the Maoris the art of tattooing is closely related to other forms of artistic expression. For instance, the same mythical source in the underworld is often attributed to both carving and tattooing. Thus the Maoris also decorated inanimate objects with *moko*, if the objects had a religious significance. The highly artistic carved wooden figures of gods or dead ancestors on meeting-houses or ceremonial buildings were lavishly decorated in this manner. The entrance gates in the palisades of fortified villages were also made in the shape of tattooed guards. All religious objects and even weapons had spiral decorations.

► Face of a Maori chief with the characteristic spiral tattoo pattern of his rank at a ceremony in Turangawaewae on the Waikato river, 1977.

Australia: the secret of the rainbow snake

Australia was settled over 40,000 years ago by the ancestors of the Aborigines, as the original inhabitants are now generally known. When the European conquest began in 1788, over five hundred small ethnic groups of hunters and gatherers lived on the continent. In the ruthless colonization that followed countless aborigines met violent deaths or died from imported diseases, and their cultures largely died with them. In the last few years an attempt has been made to compensate for the social and cultural discrimination against the aborigines by means of appropriate legislation.

There was an immense diversity among the aboriginal peoples, partly because of different environmental conditions in the areas where the various cultures lived. This is reflected in the enormous number of languages (some 300 to 500) that existed at the end of the eighteenth century; today only about fifty of the main language groups still survive. Despite the marked cultural differences between them, the aboriginal cultures do have some impressive common features, which include intricate mythologies, elaborate religious beliefs and complex social structures.

For the inhabitants of the barren semi-desert regions of Australia the main religious events were confined to the few weeks at the end of the rainy season when nature provided a surplus of food. At this time the small, nomadic local groups of a clan or a larger social unit had the opportunity to come together for major festivities. Their faces and bodies decorated with ceremonial paint and emblems symbolizing the creator beings of their mythology, they gathered at the sacred centres of their areas – pools, rocks, caves or other prominent topographical features – to celebrate initiation rites, enact rituals for promoting the fruitfulness of animals and plants and honour clan ancestors with singing and dancing. During the consecration ceremonies the novices often received wounds which left visible, ornamental scars.

Both body-painting and decorative scars are closely linked to the cultural heroes, who the aborigines believe roamed the Australian continent in a creative primeval age – the 'Dream Time' – shaping the landscape and creating all life. They left the landscape the aborigines knew, and all living creatures, as testimony to their deeds. These primeval beings could alter their shape at will and appeared sometimes as human beings, animals and plants, sometimes in the form of personified objects or that of natural phenomena such as clouds, rain or fire. One creator being that was much revered – but also feared, because of the power ascribed to it – took the form of a snake. Even today the aborigines believe it responsible for droughts. It is also responsible for the regular renewal of life in the rainy season, and, towards the end of this fertile period it often appears in the form of a rainbow – and is therefore known as the 'rainbow snake'.

The primeval creator heroes were also the forebears of individual clan groups. Members of a group therefore felt themselves akin to, and mythically connected with, the particular type of animal or plant whose form their primeval ancestor had adopted (this relationship is known as totem, from an American Indian word). The behaviour of totem group members is governed by very strict laws.

◄ Member of a group of dancers in the rain-forest area of north-east Queensland, 1988. The colours – red, black, yellow and white – symbolize, among other things, the four elements: black is the earth, and also a symbol for the traces of the fire at which the mythical ancestors camped during the Dream Time. Red combines blood, energy and fire. Yellow represents liquid, water and the marks on the back of the Great Snake Ancestor. White symbolizes the sky, the air and the stars, and represents the ancestors who went up to heaven after their work was done and became stars looking down on the earth.

Body decoration: an essential component of rituals

The designs of the dancers' face- and body-painting at a totem ritual are closely linked to the totem and usually depict a particular characteristic of that animal or object. Not only are the characteristics of these beings represented pictorially in the body-decoration, their properties or behaviour are also portrayed in the dance. The dancers can imitate animals, in particular, so brilliantly that the species of animal can be recognized just from their movements.

Mineral colours are traditionally used for the painting, with a preference for red and yellow ochre – which, in many rituals, is essential because of the powers ascribed to it. However ochre is not found in all areas and often has to be obtained by barter and transported over long distances. Other colours used are white and black; for the white paint pipeclay, gypsum or (less commonly) chalk is used, for the black soot or charcoal. Small feather balls, made from the down of indigenous birds and stuck on with blood or egg-white, give a striking three-dimensional effect. Nowadays the original mineral colours are increasingly being replaced by industrial products, very popular because the colours are brighter. Wood glue is used as a modern adhesive.

● Aboriginal painting patterns and dance costumes have specific meanings derived from mythology, which only men and women who are fully initiated know in their entirety. The patterns are not simply personal forms of identification, they are also an important part of a ritual.

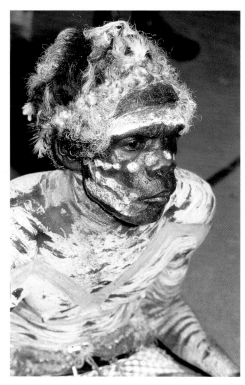

▲ Figural images were rare in Australia, and it is only in the last few decades that the aborigines of northern Australia have been producing them more frequently. The painting uses the customary local body patterns.

▲ Boys from Arnhem Land during the ten-day initiation ceremony, *c.* 1978. The geometrical pattern painted on the body, from the heart to about six inches below the navel, is the specific pattern of the clan totem. The same pattern is made on the dead body in the burial rituals. The pattern is connected, via vibrations, with the part of heaven in which the ancestor of the totem lives. This vibration helps the soul to reach the ancestor.

Introduction to the sacred knowledge

At puberty young aborigines graduate to the adult community by means of a solemn initiation. They are inducted into the group's mythical and spiritual secrets and have their first experience of the ritual acts that must be performed to secure the favour and help of the primeval forces – for aborigines believe it is only by the help of these forces that the group can survive in the infertile regions of Australia. As they grow older, they undergo further stages of initiation, until eventually they reach the highest level, when, with their now extensive knowledge of the traditions handed down, they can lead the rituals themselves. They can now make sacred logs, *tjurunga*, which must be kept hidden from the uninitiated, and they can recognize the specific body-painting schemes that the men use for each ritual, and they know all the ceremonial songs. But they always use their knowledge in the service of the community, never for their own advantage.

▲ Member of a group of dancers in Queensland, 1988. The group's paintings are based on an old pattern whose rich symbolism is explained and passed on in the initiation rites. Body-painting, like other forms of artistic expression, has a specific religious purpose. In the aborigines' attempts to revitalize their culture in recent years representative art has also been revived and kept alive with bark pictures, modern acrylic painting and sculptures with a deep symbolic content. However more and more artists are moving away from the traditional forms to commercial art.

Sacred centres of the Dream Time: birthplaces of the spirit children

The creation phase of the cultural heroes and ancestors is now known as the Dream Time. According to aboriginal mythology, the heroes of this mythical primeval age left the earth at the end of this phase. A few went up to heaven and became heavenly bodies; some turned into rocks or went into the earth, sometimes leaving behind the imprint of their bodies in rock paintings; others went back into pools. The places to which they retreated – usually prominent features of the landscape – are regarded as sacred places in which the creative force of the Dream Time is preserved.

The heroes may have lost their original forms, but the aborigines believe that they are not dead but still active and potent. They play both a passive and an active part in the lives of men, animals and plants. Passively, they ensure that the laws and rules they have laid down are followed; actively, they constantly produce new life – the aborigines believe that 'spirit children' continually emerge from the sacred centres. The spirit children are

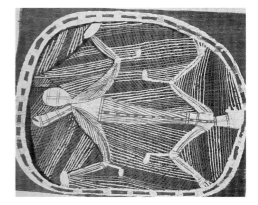

▲ Aborigines also portray mythical primeval beings in bark paintings.

▲ Aborigine with body-painting and decorative scars (1802). In many groups it is customary for young men to undergo operations such as circumcision, the removal of an incisor tooth or the piercing of the nasal septum (ornaments are subsequently worn in the hole).

the souls of the unborn, who wait to enter a woman's body and be born. They look for the body of a man and appear to him in a dream; the man then passes them on to his wife, and she becomes pregnant. Europeans, who were unaware of this belief, thought for a long time that the aborigines were ignorant of the connection between the sexual act and birth. In fact they simply attach more importance to the mental and spiritual aspects of conception than to its physical aspect.

▲ The patterns and mythical connotations of the body-painting (*kurruwari*) of Warlpiri women (Northern Territory) differ from those of the men. In the female rituals (*yawalyu*) they often relate to fertility and growth.

◄ ► The boomerang is not just for throwing in the hunt, it is also a digging-stick or a rhythmical musical instrument, and its sharp corners can be used to skin animals. This traditional tool is also represented in modern aborigine art, such as this acrylic painting (right).

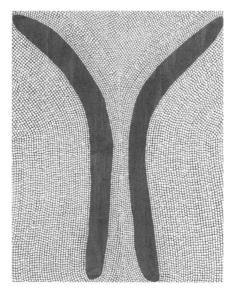

Wondjina and *mimi* spirits: aboriginal rock paintings

In the 40,000 or so years that the aborigines have lived on the Australian continent, their material civilization has changed very little. Rock paintings thousands of years old in various parts of the country show essentially the same implements, suited to the nomadic way of life, that were still used by the natives when the Europeans arrived. Stylistic changes can be detected in the portrayal of the figures in the rock paintings, but the weapons and decorations shown are very similar.

On the walls of overhanging rocks in the Kimberley district of Western Australia are pictures of strangely shaped, mouthless beings known as *wondjina*, who gave this art form its name. The aborigines believe that these paintings are sacred and that they were drawn by the primeval heroes and are in their image. They repaint the pictures regularly once a year, an act that they believe will nurture the animal and plant species on which they depend for their livelihood. Two other styles of painting have been found in rock galleries in Arnhem Land in the north of Australia, the *mimi* and X-ray styles. The *mimi* style, which is thousands of years old, is named after the narrow-limbed figures known to the aborigines as *mimi* spirits. In the more recent X-ray style the figure is portrayed with the skeleton and organs visible.

▲ *Wondjina* picture from a rock gallery in the Kimberleys, Western Australia. The first *wondjina* was found in Dream Time by Ungud, the creative primeval force, at the bottom of a waterhole. The *wondjinas* roamed the earth during the Dream Time and entered rocky places, where the imprint of their bodies can be seen.

▲ Rock drawing in eastern Arnhem Land: a group of human figures in the X-ray style, *c.* 1968.

▶ Women and fish painted in the X-ray style, Dead Adder Creek, Bala-Uru, in western Arnhem Land; painting recorded *c.* 1968. The big fish on the right of the picture is a barramunda. Painted patterns sometimes appear on the figures in the X-ray pictures. According to the aborigines the women here are wearing the body-painting for female participants in the *ngurimag-ubar* ceremony.

Oceania · Australia

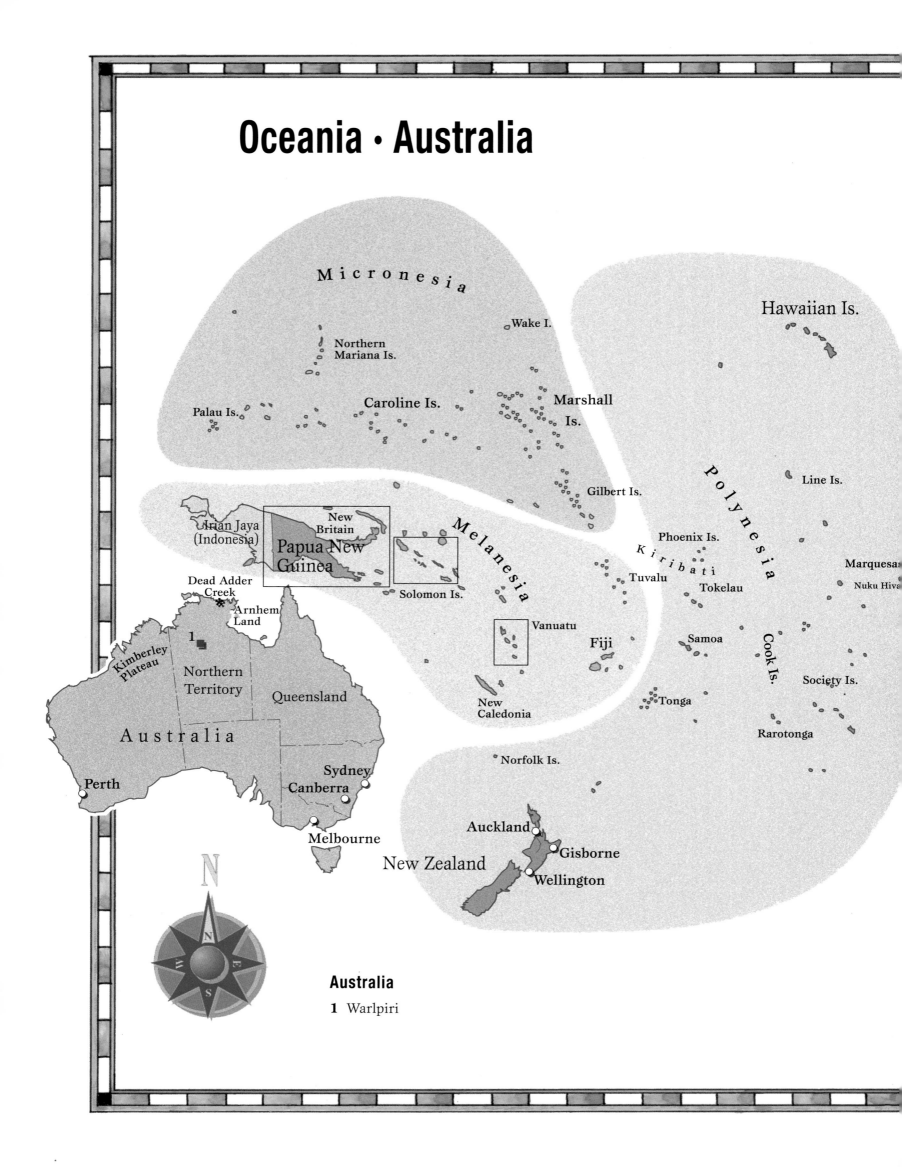

Micronesia

Hawaiian Is.

Wake I.

Northern
Mariana Is.

Palau Is.

Caroline Is.

Marshall
Is.

Line Is.

Gilbert Is.

Polynesia

Irian Jaya
(Indonesia)

New
Britain

Melanesia

Phoenix Is.

Papua New
Guinea

Kiribati

Marquesas

Dead Adder
Creek

Solomon Is.

Tuvalu

Nuku Hiva

Tokelau

Arnhem
Land

Vanuatu

Samoa

Cook Is.

Kimberley
Plateau

1

Fiji

Northern
Territory

Queensland

Society Is.

New
Caledonia

Tonga

Rarotonga

Australia

Norfolk Is.

Sydney
Canberra

Perth

Melbourne

Auckland

Gisborne

New Zealand

Wellington

N

Australia

1 Warlpiri

A Papua New Guinea highlander paints himself for a ceremony.

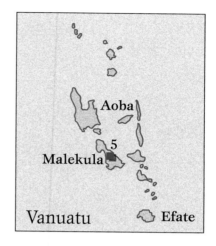

Vanuatu

Aoba

Malekula 5

Efate

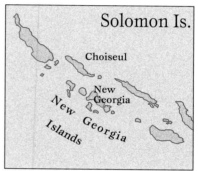

Solomon Is.

Choiseul

New Georgia

New Georgia Islands

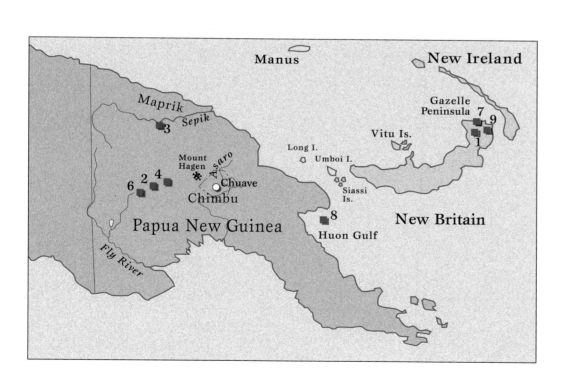

Manus

New Ireland

Maprik

Sepik 3

Mount Hagen

Asaro

Chuave

Chimbu

6 2 4

Papua New Guinea

Fly River

Long I.

Umboi I.

Siassi Is.

8

Huon Gulf

Gazelle Peninsula 7 9

1

Vitu Is.

New Britain

Papua New Guinea and Vanuatu

1 Baining
2 Huli
3 Iatmul
4 Mendi
5 Namba
6 Samo
7 Sulka
8 Tami
9 Tolai

Africa: the diversity of shapes, the power of colours

In many African societies people use their own skin as another medium for their creativity and artistic talents, cutting into its surface like wood-carvers and changing its nature like sculptors. Their faces and bodies are the canvas on which African painters display their art. Decorated skin turns the body into a living sculpture and elevates it to a work of art; its conscious design marks it as an expression of human civilization, which, through art, is firmly distinguished from the unformed nature that surrounds it. The rules of this art are laid down and handed on by the community.

The aesthetics of painting, scarification and tattooing can only be fully appreciated when seen against their social and religious background. Skin-decoration shows a person's social rank and history, where he comes from and whom he belongs to, and through it he also professes his religious faith. Ceremonial patterns transport him out of his secular everyday life and into the spiritual world; they protect him from negative influences and link him to his forebears. As a system of symbols the decorations do not simply proclaim the values and ideals of a society, they pass them on and reinforce them.

◀ The young men of the Nuba in East Africa are famous throughout the world for the extraordinary creativity of their sensational body art.

113

Red: the colour of life and death

For many African societies red is a deeply symbolic colour. However, it is impossible to attribute to it a general and unvarying significance, for red has different connotations in different cultures. Its interpretation also depends on who it is that is making use of the symbolism of the colour, on what occasion and, above all, when.

For instance, red is often associated with human blood. But this can lead to a wide variety of interpretations – for some the colour of blood is the colour of life, joy and health, whilst elsewhere it signifies death, grief and transience. In many Central African societies healers paint the sick with red ochre to stimulate the life force – but for the Ashanti in Ghana, on the other hand, red is the colour of mourning.

The diversity of African languages also makes it generally difficult to judge colours. The way in which people see and describe colours is often different, and in many cases the classification of shades also varies considerably. Sometimes the words for colours in African languages also take into account other properties: the nature of the surface, or particular shadings or patterns. As a result, colour concepts arise that have no equivalent in European languages and can only be expressed by means of paraphrase.

◄ A statue of a drummer that plays an important role in the circumcision rites of the Yaka in central Africa. Red is often used for initiation rites, together with white. They can symbolize either death or life.

▲ Masks with a red background are used in rites of passage among the Biombo in Zaire.

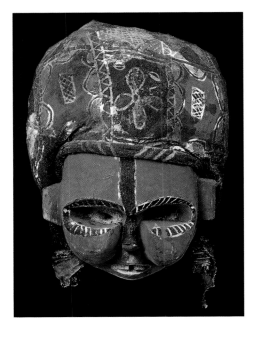

◀ Colours are often associated with specific gods or other supernatural beings. This red mask from the Zairean Nkanu, for instance, symbolizes the spirit Kakungu, who protects humans from harm by healing the sick and warding off natural disasters.

▲ Decorated Hemba woman dancing. In Africa, red colouring is obtained from mineral, vegetable and animal substances; nowadays industrial colours tend to be increasingly used. The colours and their various shades have spiritual and social connotations.

White: a link with the supernatural

In Africa, how colours are used and what they symbolize depends on culture and situation and is also related to historical and social conditions. It is difficult, therefore, to establish a symbolic meaning of the colour white that is uniformly valid.

For many African groups white – especially when used for ritual and ceremonial purposes – symbolizes the link with the spirits of the ancestors and other supernatural beings. But even here there is a differentiation to be made, because in some societies white is associated with frightening spirits, whilst elsewhere (or on other occasions) it symbolizes friendly and helpful spirits.

White paint is frequently used in the initiation rites at which boys and girls are recognized by the community as adults. The initiates are often dusted or painted from head to foot with white, which in this context is both a symbol of purity and at the same time a sign of the novice's transitional state between the human and supernatural worlds. In many societies white also has a purifying, healing and protective effect.

In body-painting white is often combined with other colours, and the juxtaposition usually expresses spiritual and emotional contrasts. For instance, white can represent gentleness, whereas red symbolizes aggressiveness. White colouring material is generally made from kaolin, light clay, flour or ground mussel shells.

◄ In many African societies boys and girls are painted white at initiation ceremonies as a visible sign of their removal from the world of humans.

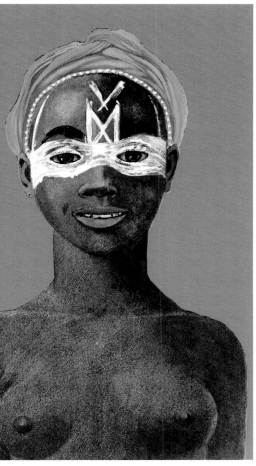

● Lobi girls in Burkina Faso are painted with white skeleton patterns during initiation rites. This is to show that the ancestors are not completely dead but come back to life through the young women.

Stylization: the human and non-human worlds

In most African societies the patterns and ornaments on masks are not necessarily the same as those used for body art. In fact the nature and scale of the decoration often differs considerably. Body-painting, tattooed patterns and scarification have social and ritual significance, but at the same time they still have to satisfy the human need for beauty. Thus in body art attention is drawn to certain parts of the body and their attractions are

▲ The children of the mythical ancestor Woot and other prehistoric beings are often represented in the masks of the Zairean Bakuba.

◄ The features on this Batetela mask from central Africa denote non-human status. The masks and the costumes that go with them are kept in total seclusion. The wearer is completely concealed in the costume, and his appearance is intended to alarm and intimidate the audience.

emphasized. With mask patterns, on the other hand, the intention is often precisely the opposite: they are meant to be remote from the mortal world and show that the beings portrayed are outside human society. Heavily stylized, so as to produce an alienating effect, they embody non-human beings such as spirits, mythical figures or animals.

▲ This nineteenth-century male mask of the Bakuba (Zaire) was used during the young men's initiation rites. The chameleon eyes indicate that it is the mythical being Mulwala.

◄ This secret-society mask from the central African Songye people has a grooved surface. Secret societies often had a police and judicial function, maintaining public order and ensuring that community's rules were obeyed. The authority of these associations was often linked to fear and respect for tutelary spirits, symbolized in special rites by masked dancers.

Permanent amulets: the tattoos of Berber women

In many North African Berber groups the women, in particular, bear a range of tattoos, the patterns and techniques being passed down from mother to daughter. The patterns are decorative, but in many cases their main purpose is to ward off supernatural forces that might harm human beings; the tattoos act as a kind of talisman, safeguarding the health and well-being of the wearer.

Berbers attribute illnesses not only to physical causes but also to the effect of non-human forces. Children and those in a transitional stage of life in which their physical and mental state is weakened – such as puberty, marriage, pregnancy or childbirth – are particularly susceptible to malicious spirits. At such critical times there is also a fear of the negative forces of the Evil Eye, which malevolent humans might use to cause illness and death.

Because the harmful forces prefer to enter people through the bodily orifices, these have to be specially protected. The women therefore tattoo their faces in particular, although protective and curative tattoos and paintings are also found on other parts of the body that cannot be protected by clothing at all times.

◄ This young Berber woman from the High Atlas is effectively protected by the tattoos on her nose, under her mouth and around her eyes. The silver jewellery characteristic of this region, often ornamented with such natural phenomena as the sun and the moon, also has a talismanic function. (Photograph, 1980)

▲ The intricate and finely painted patterns on the hands are applied before a wedding, for instance. The women use henna dye, which is believed to give strong protection.

121

The *siyala*: decoration and talisman of female fertility

There has been much speculation about whether the tattooed patterns of the Berbers might in former times have been a kind of 'tribal mark' to identify members of a local or kinship group. There are certainly regional differences in the decorations, and the actual technique also varies, but there is little solid evidence to support this theory.

The motifs found in skin-decoration are similar to the ornamentation on carpets, textiles and the walls of houses in the northern regions of the Sahara, and the basic elements used are generally very simple: crosses, dots, straight lines and triangles, along with stylized representations of date palms or palm branches. The Berbers believe this ornamentation, known as *siyala*, to be particularly effective in averting harm and promoting fertility. The *siyala* is therefore seen as the 'most feminine' of patterns, and it is the one most often used on girls at puberty. The palm, a symbol of fertility, relates to the children the young woman hopes to have. It is particularly clear from the *siyala* that tattooing and painting in Africa often has a triple function: to embellish, to destroy negative influences and to increase the strength of positive forces.

◄ (Top): The eyes are regarded as the bodily orifice most at risk. They are therefore surrounded with protective ornamentation. Silver jewellery also wards off evil spirits.

◄ (Bottom): Berber women use the *siyala* pattern not only on their faces but also on the backs of their hands. It may be either painted on or tattooed.

▲ Protection is also needed for bare feet and heels. In this case the traditional pattern prevents hostile forces from working evil magic on the 'soul material' that is left behind in the footprints.

The Wodabe bridegrooms' parade: male beauty contest

The Wodabe, sometimes known as the Bororo, are nomadic herdsmen living in the Republic of Niger and neighbouring regions. For most of the year they traverse the barren regions of the southern Sahara in small groups, moving from one grazing ground to another with their herds of camels, cattle and donkeys. Once a year – in the rainy season, when there is enough vegetation to feed many animals in one place – the Wodabe gather in large numbers. At this important meeting they get to know each other, consolidate existing relationships, forge new links and hold feasts. For the young people, in particular, this is their main opportunity to find a partner.

The one-week *geerewol* festival with its 'bridegrooms' parade' dance is the centre-point of these large gatherings. On this occasion the Wodabe men make a special effort to enhance their appearance; they spend hours adorning themselves with paint and make-up in front of small hand mirrors to make themselves look as desirable as possible to the women. The dance is actually a competition in which the men are obliged to, and also anxious to, display their physical attractions. They further enhance the effect of the make-up by exaggerated facial expressions, rolling their eyes and puffing out their cheeks. The winner chosen by the women is ultimately picked for his facial expression and dance movements.

◄ When they make themselves up men follow their society's idea of beauty: light skin, high forehead, narrow nose. The lips and the area around the eyes are also blackened to bring out the white of the teeth and eyes.

▲ Unlike painting, which is used with jewellery and richly decorated clothing to enhance a young man's beauty, the tattoos seen here are chiefly protective. The triangles at the corners of the mouth are believed to protect against the feared 'evil eye' from malevolent humans.

Surma stick-fights in Ethiopia: duels as conflict management

The Surma are a pastoral society living around the Omo river in south-western Ethiopia. The young unmarried men come together several times a year from various villages for the *donga* stick-fights: duels in which the opponent must be put out of action with a hard wooden stick, no more than two metres long, in the shortest possible time. The fights are usually so quick, determined and ruthless that most only last for a few seconds.

On these occasions the men decorate their faces and bodies with sweeping linear patterns that proclaim their origin and confirm their membership of a group (each represents a particular village). The main purpose of the painting, however, is to emphasize the individual's strength and intimidate his opponent before the fight. For the fight itself a kind of protective uniform is worn to prevent the most serious injuries to head, arms and shoulders. Thus few are ever killed, despite the furious force of the blows

● Surma men preparing for the *donga* stick fight. They cover their bodies with a layer of water and chalk, on which they then make a pattern of lines with their fingers.

– especially as the referees intervene immediately if the situation becomes critical.

For the young men the stick-fights are a socially acceptable way of attracting the attention and favour of unmarried women. They also create a sense of communal identity within the villages and direct the potential for conflict between neighbouring groups into controlled channels.

Attributes of recognition among the Mursi and the Bumi

The Mursi and the Bumi also come from the Omo valley of south-west Ethiopia. They are agriculturalists who live mainly from cattle-rearing and rainy-season farming; alluvial land flooded by the river is also used. Cattle are a yardstick of wealth and a food source, and they also have an important role as valuable barter goods when crops fail.

Since the early 1970s, in particular, this region of Ethiopia has regularly been ravaged by devastating droughts and famines. These natural disasters have increasingly caused serious conflicts between cattle-owning societies in the Omo valley, with constant raids and counter-raids as they fight to survive.

The Omo valley groups are famous for the diversity of the decorative scars, arranged in aesthetic patterns, with which they ornament their faces and bodies. These prestigious marks are often closely linked to meaningful and complex rituals in which hunting and killing play an important part.

◄ The scars on the arms and bodies of the Mursi are often a record of personal achievements – mainly feats of bravery in battle or outstanding skill at hunting. The coveted marks enhance the social prestige of their wearer.

► Bumi men adorn their faces with scar patterns and wear multi-coloured hair decorations made of clay. Often a macrame holder, into which peacock feathers can be stuck on special occasions, is also worked into the elaborate coiffure.

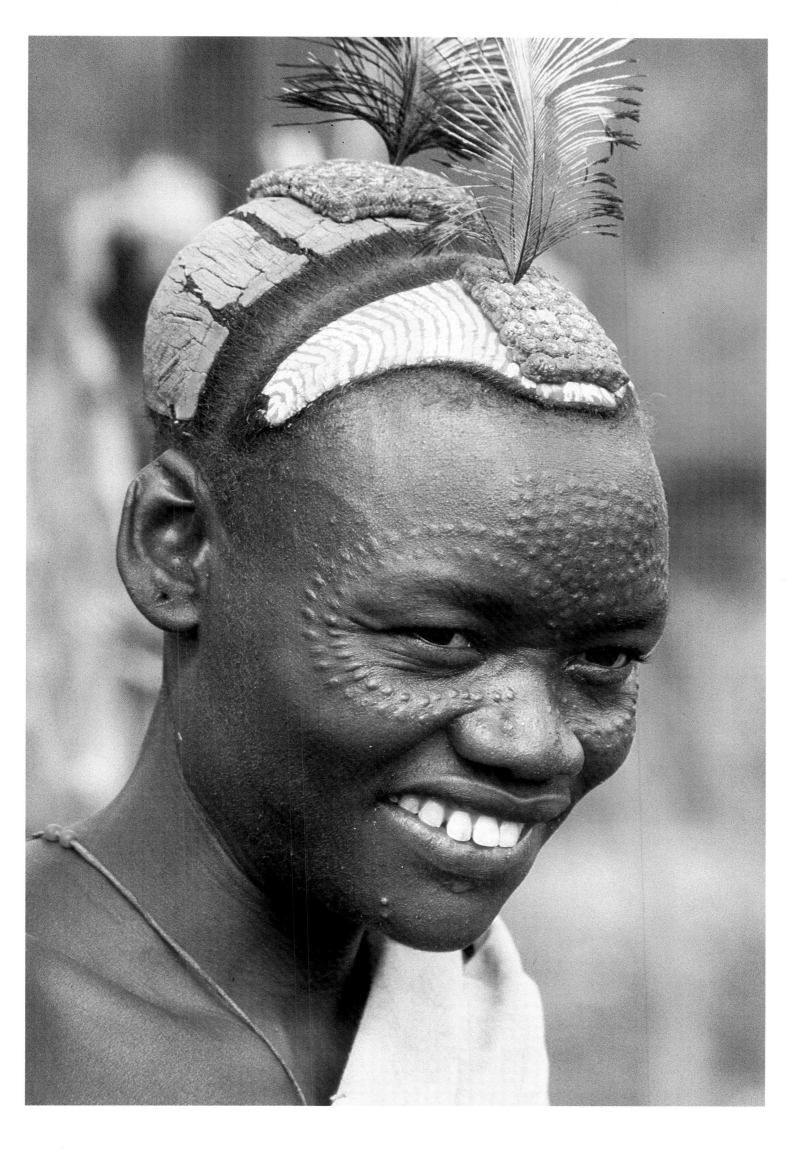

The transient art of the Ethiopian Karo

▲ Before dancing the Karo paint their bodies with patterns that often symbolize particular animals. Here a pattern in white chalk was made to simulate the plumage of a guinea-fowl.

East African pastoral societies are generally divided into 'age groups'. In the course of their life men, and often also women, belong to the group appropriate to their age, which has particular responsibilities and behaviour models. In most communities there are three age groups for the males – childhood, warriors and elders – and the transition between them is usually accompanied by initiation rites. The boys look after the herds and perform minor tasks in the village, while the warriors, who protect the community, generally have no commitments at this stage of their lives. The elders take the

political decisions, and only they are allowed to start a family and begin building up their own herds. The girls progress more directly from childhood into adulthood as marriageable women.

There are specific forms of body-painting and scarification for men and women at all these stages, for instance among the Karo, herdsmen and farmers in south-western Ethiopia. For some years now the Karo have been facing enormous changes: the spread of the drought has intensified conflicts between the groups in south-west Ethiopia, and with modern weapons violent political clashes are now on a

► The Karo often wear elaborate clay coiffures, as well as painting their faces with ochre, yellow and white. The clay is applied straight to the skin on the head and dusted or painted with various colours.

dramatic scale. But their elaborate painting has also brought far-reaching changes, for some of the Karo now make their living as photographic models for the growing influx of tourists.

● On Bambara (Bamana) figures from Mali, this Kuyu ritual staff from Congo and
royal statuette from the N'Dengese in Central Africa numerous decorative scar patt
are reproduced with great accuracy.

Symbols of fulfilment, social values and ideals

In many African societies the people decorate themselves with striking scars, ornamenting their bodies with a wide variety of patterns. The purpose and function of these important body markings can only be understood in the context of the social background. In many cases the scarification denotes a particular age group, but elsewhere it might signify membership of a particular local group or kinship.

Each stage in a person's life is associated with scars: children are often given the first incisions immediately after birth. Further scarifications are then added at regular intervals – in the case of women, for instance, on their first menstruation, after the birth of the first child or after they finish breast-feeding.

The painful decorations are seen as a way of improving physical appearance, and they are erotic in their sensual connotations. The main purpose of scars is to ensure success with the opposite sex, because a person is not a 'real man' or 'real woman' without them. In many societies people without visible incisions are seen as anti-social and looked down on as cowards and outsiders.

▶ The Kaleri women of Nigeria are very proud of their decorative scars, in the application of which they have to undergo considerable pain. These signs of their femininity make them attractive and desirable.

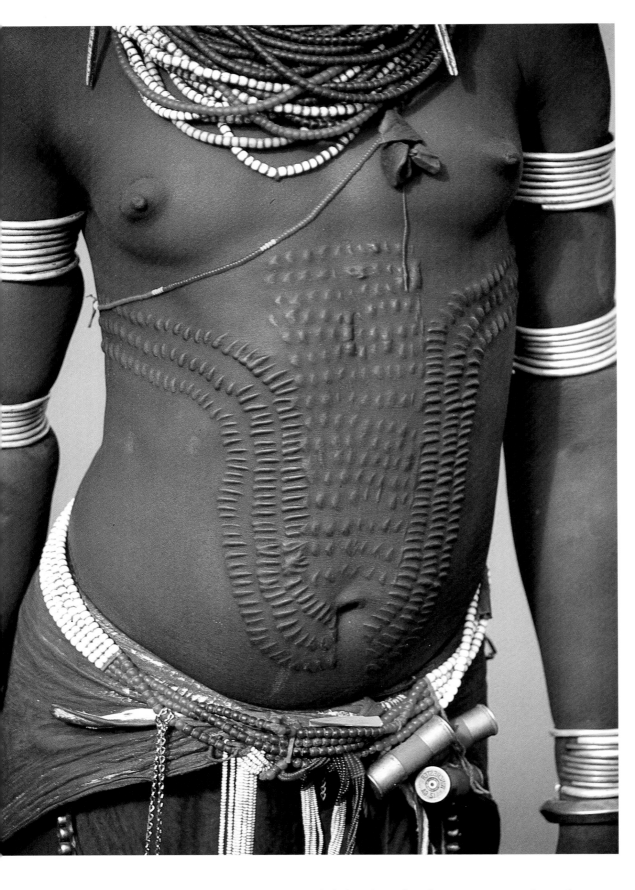

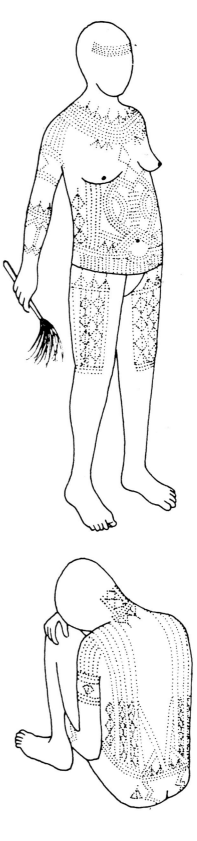

▲ Unlike the men's painting, which fades after a few days, Karo women in south-west Ethiopia have permanent scar patterns that indicate their age and status.

Lifelong markings: testimony to personal experience

Scars are marks that document and record important stages in a person's life. But the absence of skin-decoration, too, can indicate a person's social status, for expert practitioners are often too costly for everyone to be able to afford their services.

By no means all scars have a symbolic meaning or social implications. Many are simply the result of medical treatment – blood-letting or the introduction of medicinal and protective substances into the skin – or the marks of burns deliberately administered to particular parts of a sick person's body to stimulate the immune system. The Nuba, for instance, make incisions over the eyes to improve eyesight, while incisions in the temples are believed to relieve headaches.

◄ The women of the Ga'anda in Nigeria undergo a programme of scarification extending over several years. From the age of about five, scars are incised on specific parts of their bodies in a traditionally prescribed order. The operation is carried out by experts, generally older women. Young women are not considered to be adult and marriageable until these designs, known as *hleeta*, are completed.

The drawing shows the sequence: the first scars are on the stomach, with later incisions made on the forehead and then the forearms, the back of the neck, the waist, the buttocks and hips and the upper arms. Finally the decoration of the whole body is completed with eight different patterns.

▲ The scars on the back of this Nuba woman from the Sudan show that she has had at least one child.

Living sculptures: variations on an ancient theme

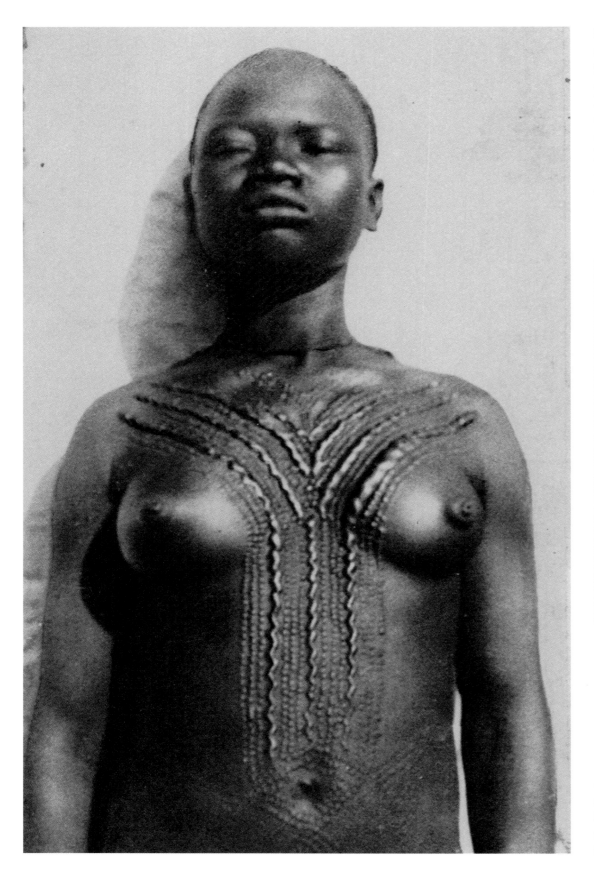

Scarification is usually carried out by specially trained experts, recognized for their skills, who may be either men or women. The technique varies very little: small cuts are made with razors or thorns, and the wounds are then covered with charcoal. When they have healed, raised scars are visible, sometimes showing the blue-black colouring of the incised lines.

▲ This man's scarification in regular patterns make his arm look like a carved work of art. (1928 photo)

◀ This photo from the colonial period, c. 1925, is of a Mbaye woman from what is now Chad. The deep scars are made by repeated incisions and by irritating the fresh wound with small foreign bodies.

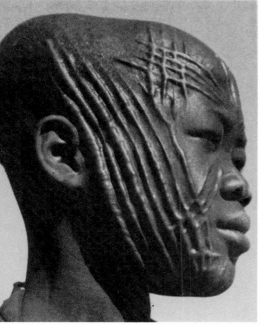

◄ Many African governments have now banned so-called 'tribal marks', scars denoting membership of a particular local group or kinship. But even in the countries where it is banned the practice continues in secret. These two photos show men from present-day Chad and Zaire.

▲ The scars on this Tabwa woman, from what is now Zaire, symbolize fertility. The arrangement of teardrop-shaped scars around a central point is typical.

The fantastic 'uniforms' of the Nuba

In the Nuba mountains in southern Sudan live about fifty different farming communities numbering almost half a million people, now known by the generic name of Nuba. Their main livelihood is farming, supplemented by cattle-rearing.

In some of the south-eastern Nuba groups the colours of the body-painting and special hairstyles show a person's age group. A distinction is made between the older boys, who guard the herds, the young men, who mainly work in the fields and are initiated into the community's religion, and the elders, who also work in the fields. The men who lead the rituals belong to the last age group.

In the villages of Kau, Nyaro and Fungor, in particular, the young men have developed body- and face-painting into a fine art. The paintings are done not just by particularly gifted artists but by all the men between the ages of seventeen and thirty. Thus body art is a kind of 'uniform' for each age group, embodying the hopes of the community. The limited life of the painted colours and forms reflects the transience of youthful strength, health and beauty. The exceptionally fine and artistic decorations must, however, stand up to the critical scrutiny of a public that is only too ready to scorn and mock unsuccessful patterns and colour combinations.

● The painted face masks of young Nuba men take many hours of concentrated work. They are remarkable mainly for the balance of colours and patterns. (1976 photo)

Unlimited power of expression

Contemporaries in the same village district usually decorate themselves together. They take it in turns to embellish each others' backs and swap paints. When they visit another village, the host provides oil and paints. Despite this close collaboration between the young men, no two patterns are the same.

For the Nuba the hairstyle is very important. As soon as boys join the first age group they wear their hair like a small cap with a tuft on the scalp, and they keep this crest all their life until they are admitted to the elders' group – old men shave their heads. Young Nuba men have particularly elaborate hairstyles. Their hair 'caps' are bigger than those of the boys and can be divided into sections. The scalp is sometimes decorated with a continuous tuft from forehead to neck.

To avoid spoiling their appearance, the decorated men even have to suffer a certain amount of discomfort while sleeping, because the carefully constructed hairstyle could be ruined by a careless movement during the night. They try to prevent such damage by using neck supports when they sleep, so as to leave their heads unsupported and their coiffures uncompressed.

● Colours and patterns are combined in endless permutations. The general impression is rounded off by the hair. No two painted face masks are the same.

The rules of colour: a man's career

The use of colours is subject to strict rules and linked to membership of particular age groups. Red and white are the first colours that an older boy is allowed to use, from the age of about eight. Once he becomes a young man he may also use yellow. Black decorations are not normally permitted until he is officially initiated into this age group a year or two later. These conventions is strictly monitored by the Nuba, and if a younger man uses a colour to which he is not entitled, he is punished by the elders.

To conserve body heat and for cleanliness, men and women usually oil themselves twice a day – normally morning and evening – whether they are planning to decorate themselves again or removing an existing decoration. Often the paintings represent animals, with their shape adapted to the human anatomy. Particular features of the animal appear on the corresponding parts of the person's body, for instance leopard-skin markings on the back and chest. Animals may also be represented by symbols: antelopes for instance by a narrow stripe over the eyes, or jackals by marks on the artist's legs.

● At least in the early decades of this century, each family had its own sites from which it obtained ochre earth, used as a colouring matter. For some time now, however, most of the colours have come from a single region.

● The greyish white background for the face-painting comes from chalky rock and freshwater mussel shells.

Bizarre facial decorations

The face is not always painted in the same way as the body. For instance, the decoration can symbolize two different kinds of animal, or abstract and figurative pictures be used side by side. Each body-decoration requires the careful application of an oil base beforehand. Until a few years ago the oil was derived from either animal or plant sources; nowadays it is mainly bought from traders.

● Facial patterns are made with the fingers, small sticks, straws or tufts of grass. Small carved stamps are also used.

Prescribed patterns and shades of colour: women's markings

By comparison with the extravagant paintings of the young men, the scar patterns of Nuba women seem relatively subdued. The scarification reflects their role in society and indicates their responsibilities. In fact exactly when particular parts of a woman's body may be decorated with the appropriate patterns are strictly laid down.

Scarification is applied in three stages. Firstly, on the torso at the age of about ten, and under the breasts after the first menstruation; after the first child is weaned further scarifications are added on the back, arms and legs. However, it is not only scars that denote a woman's status. For instance, only girls who have not yet been pregnant normally cover their whole bodies with a mixture of oil and ochre. And a woman's hair is shaved at the initial stage of pregnancy and only allowed to grow back again after the birth. The colour of her skirt shows whether a woman is expecting her first child, has weaned it, or has reached the menopause.

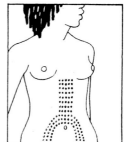 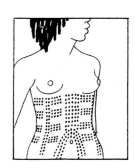

◀ The different shades of colour on girls' oiled skins denote the group they belong to. The oil is mixed with ochre in a shade indicating the girl's paternal clan.

● Skilled women carry out the scarification. The skin is first raised with a thorn. Incisions are then made with a sharp knife or razor blade. Sometimes

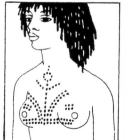 

women lose a great deal of blood in the process. Spreading oil, flour and herbs on the wounds helps to relieve the pain.

Festive Dinka and Surma painting

Amongst the Dinka in southern Sudan important decisions affecting the community are taken in each village by a council of the adult men – there is no higher political authority. Individual groups in this pastoral society normally spend the six-month rainy season in one place; in the dry season they move between several grazing grounds and camps with their herds. In the last few years the Dinka have suffered a great deal from the

▲ ▼ Dinka have a close relationship with their cattle and paint themselves with a mixture of dung-ash and cow's urine. To make the patterns adhere to the skin better, they first cover their whole bodies with grease.

civil war in the southern Sudan and from attacks by modern slave traders.

Like many pastoral societies in East Africa the Dinka are divided into age groups. When they become adults the young men have deep horn-shaped or parallel lines cut into their foreheads. This sign of maturity shows that the wearers were brave enough to undergo the painful process. Both men and women decorate their bodies and faces for important social occasions.

▶ Surma girls having their faces and bodies painted for the men's *donga* stick fights.

148

The 'pearls' of the Shilluk and the Punu

The Shilluk are cattle herders living in southern Sudan. Their political structure differs considerably from that of the Dinka, for all Shilluk groups worship the same sacred king, whose functions are chiefly religious and ritual, though also political.

Many Shilluk decorate their foreheads with pearl-like scars, made when they are children by pulling the skin up with a fish-hook and then cutting it off with a sharp knife. This type of scarification has now come to denote membership of Shilluk society.

▲ ► A circlet of scarring on the forehead is a typical facial decoration among the Shilluk in the Sudan.

◄ This Punu dance mask from Gabon represents the spirit of a dead person. The geometrical or floral decorations on the forehead and between the eyes and ears, reproducing scarification marks, are characteristic of this type of mask, worn by stilt walkers. Their shape is reminiscent of the Shilluk scars.

▲ These Kikuyu dancers from central Kenya decorate their bodies with a mixture of fat and chalk, painting the geometrical patterns on the skin with their fingers.

The Samburu and the Kikuyu: tradition and change

◄ Amongst the Samburu in Kenya members of the warrior class dress themselves up magnificently. The ochre paint on the face, neck and chest, the ivory ear pegs and the hair elaborately styled with animal fat are typical.

The Kikuyu live in the central highlands of Kenya. Numbering about three million, they are the largest ethnic group in this East African country. For a long time most Kikuyu were farmers and traders; nowadays they work as entrepreneurs, civil servants, employees and manual workers in Kenya's towns. (Jomo Kenyatta, Kenya's first President after independence, was a Kikuyu.) Until around the turn of the century Kikuyu society was based on an age-group system, but with the dramatic changes in the past few decades this has largely died out.

The Samburu, famous for their elaborate ochre body-painting, also live in Kenya. As in most other pastoral societies in East Africa, among the Samburu this form of body decoration is confined to the age group of the young independent men. Their imposing appearance is, however, in stark contrast to their influence in the community and their say in its affairs; it is the older men, inconspicuous in appearance, who have the power and status.

Symbol of youth: Masai body decoration

The Masai are cattle herders living in Kenya and Tanzania. For a long time scientists and development aid workers failed to understand their cleverly devised economic system, ideally suited to the natural environment of the Serengeti plateau. They were unfairly criticized because their herds were reared primarily for ritual, religious and social purposes and were therefore not economically sound. We now know that cattle as a source of meat and milk play an important part in feeding the population. In times of drought, in particular, the large herds constitute a food reserve.

The ceremony at which young men pass from the warrior group to the ranks of elders is particularly impressive. A special camp is built for the five-day rites, and often several hundred men gather for the occasion – which is held only every seven to fourteen years. The paintings emphasize the health and fitness of the young male body. The end and climax of the ceremony is the shaving of the young men's heads. This dramatically signals the end of their independent life, as they lose the hair decoration that, during their time as warriors, was a symbol of pride and unfettered youth.

● Masai warriors spend a long time painting their bodies, drawing the patterns in the paint with their fingers, sticks or tufts of grass while it is still wet. The patterns often symbolize deeds of heroism, for instance a particularly successful hunt.

◄▲ Most Masai girls marry soon after their initiation and circumcision. The person who gives the bride away and the bride's family have ochre rubbed into their faces and necks for the occasion.

Marriage and the end of youth

► The end of the warrior phase of life is marked by the *olngesherr* ceremony, at which the young men are finally accepted into the ranks of the elders. Many Masai decorate themselves with blue and red face-paint for the ceremony.

Royal decorations of the Mangbetu

In the eighteenth and nineteenth centuries the Mangbetu, settled mainly in the north east of Zaire, had a powerful military apparatus. This gave the leaders, in particular, access to tributes exacted from neighbouring groups. They also controlled the ivory and copper trade in the region.

Men and women rubbed their bodies with a mixture of redwood and palm oil, giving the skin a reddish glint. Women's faces and bodies were decorated with scars and with painting. The patterns were generally removed after two days and replaced with new ones, applied either freehand or with small wooden stamps.

The elaborate painting indicated the social superiority of the Mangbetu elite. The stylized patterns are also found on, for instance, carefully modelled wooden figures that had been made for the nobles.

▲ The Mangbetu have developed the imaginative designs of head ornamentation into a fine art.

► A skull tapering sharply towards the back is the Mangbetu ideal of beauty. Heads are shaped from babyhood to achieve this. (Drawing from a 1937 photograph)

▲ The back and legs of this Mangbetu woman are decorated not with tattoos or scarification but with indelible plant sap. (1937)

▲ Queen Mutubani, over sixty years old, has her body painted by serving girls, a task which takes several hours. The patterns are mainly geometric motifs, such as stars, crosses, dots and intersecting lines. The photograph dates from 1910.

159

'Dying and growing up': the Xhosa and the Fingo

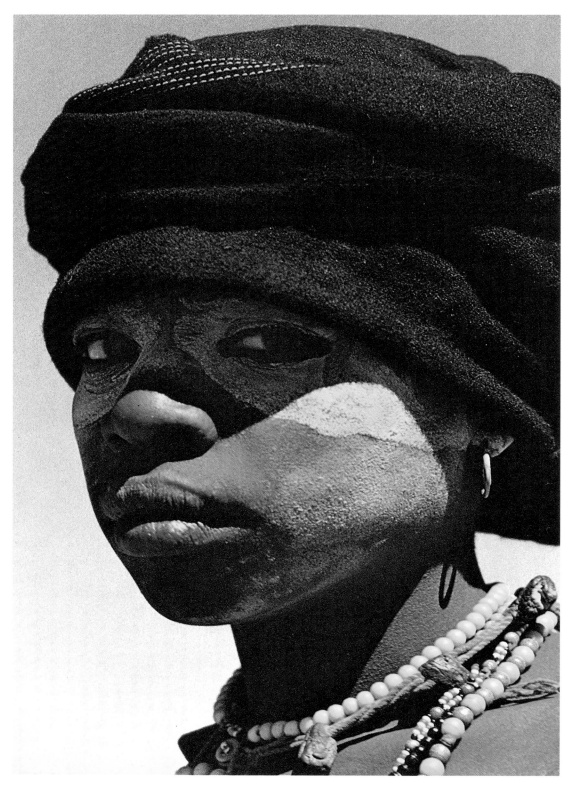

▲ Among the Fingo, neighbours of the Xhosa, young women have white decorations around their eyes and on their cheeks. This symbolizes the hope that they will soon bear a child and is a visible sign of their desire for fertility.

The Xhosa are indigenous to the eastern Cape of South Africa, primarily what are now Transkei and Ciskei. For a long time most of the population lived by cattle-rearing and farming. Now that South Africa has become industrialized, however, many Xhosa work as labourers in the mines or factories.

When they are about to become adults the young Xhosa are even now isolated in small groups in bush camps away from their homes. There, far from their families, they are circumcised, have to speak in a special ritual language and are only allowed certain foods. They paint their bodies white from head to foot, repainting them every day. This signifies that during their initiation they are outside society, suffering as it were a 'social' death. At the same time the colour symbolizes a drawing closer to their ancestors, who grant or deny fertility to people, land and cattle, keep diseases away from family members and protect them against enemies. At this time the young men always carry on their wrists small receptacles containing the white paint, which is made from ground chalk mixed with stream water.

After three or four months, when the circumcision wounds have healed, the boys return to the community of the living, and the white paint is washed off. An aged dignitary then anoints them, and they are admitted to the warrior age group with a stroke of the spear – although nowadays this has no military significance. After that the young adults are given instruction on the rights and duties involved in starting a family and receive gifts from their parents and sweethearts.

▲ Young Xhosa live outside society for several months for the rites that make them into adults. The white painting symbolizes their exceptional status and separates them from society and the world of the living.

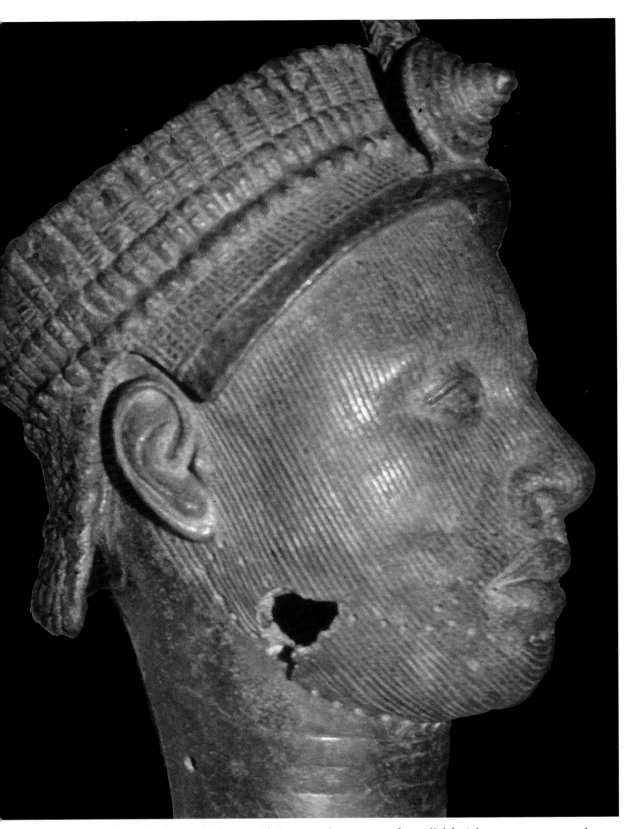

Ife bronze heads

Since the beginning of this century a number of terracotta and metal sculptures, dating from before the seventeenth century, have been dug up in and around Ife, a town in southern Nigeria. The finds have included representations of human bodies with evenly balanced scarifications, and occasionally faint traces of black, white and red paint can still be seen in the grooves of these scars. The idealized naturalism of these sculptures, unique in Africa, has created a sensation all over the world.

The city of Ife is the sacred city of the Yoruba, to which most of the kingdoms in the area can be traced. The meaning of the fine scarifications on the figures is a mystery. Their classification as 'tribal marks' is unconfirmed, because such scars are unknown amongst the present-day Yoruba, although, since the people they represent were probably dignitaries, scars might well have been a sign of their high social status. The purpose of the heads has also not yet been established, and we can only speculate.

As well as the fine lines on the faces, many of the Ife heads have very prominent welt-like scars; again their meaning is unknown. It has been assumed up to now that they were a form of commemorative head on the altars of deceased dignitaries. Only future archaeological research can provide answers to these questions. It is likely, however, that countless objects still remain to be unearthed in Nigeria.

▲ In the world-famous Ife bronzes the pattern of parallel facial scars accentuates the delicate modelling of the heads.

▲ The Ife heads are striking proof that bronze-casting was already a fine art in Africa in early times, and its products were in no way inferior to European masterpieces of the time.

Yoruba: the body as reflection of inner qualities

Most of the eighteen million or so Yoruba have now settled in south-west Nigeria. Until the beginning of the European colonial period they were organized into about fifty independent kingdoms, headed by sacred kings.

Yoruba body art is chiefly for aesthetic purposes. It also reflects the social structure and the view of the world and concepts of human existence on which it is based.

The *kolo* markings – scars decorating the body and face – play a particularly important role in this respect. The scarifications show a person's inner qualities, such as bravery, and reveal his state of mind, for instance grief or pain. The incisions are made by experienced specialists with a Y-shaped double-edged knife. As soon as the skin is scratched, pigments such as powdered charcoal are rubbed into the wounds to colour the scar patterns produced. The scars have to be made perfectly and with great care, because too deep a cut makes a large wound that leaves ugly scars. The Yoruba worship Ogun, the god of iron, as the tutelary deity of body artists.

By no means all Yoruba scars are symbolic, however. Some are simply the relics of previous medical treatments, in which the skin has been scratched to introduce medicinal substances into the body.

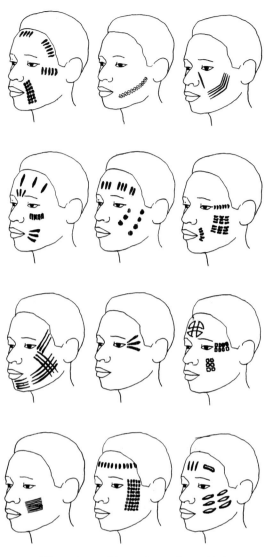

▲ There is a wide variety of motifs in Yoruba *kolo* markings, which include representational patterns such as animals and plants, as well as geometrical ones. Scars may also be in the shape of status symbols or everyday objects, or they may have religious significance: for instance symbols of the thunder god Shango. The scarifications often also contain references to proverbs or epigrams.

◄ The scars worn by marriageable women often indicate their willingness and determination to endure the pain of childbirth.

► This carved wood veranda post in the form of a human figure was painted black and white with oil paints from Europe. It depicts a mother and child. The dark facial decorations might be *kolo* scars. (c. 1920)

Luluwa: the marks of dignity, hope and vitality

Amongst the Luluwa of Zaire decorative scars are both aesthetic and symbolic. Primarily emphasizing the health and beauty of the skin, they also reflect a woman's exemplary moral and physical attributes. Scar markings are often found on Luluwa ancestor figures, which reproduce them extraordinarily precisely.

Luluwa women who have lost several children through miscarriages or infant mortality usually join the *bwanga bwa cibola* cult. After acceptance, they have to conform to a specific code of behaviour and dietary rules, once they become pregnant again. They are also given motherhood figures to protect the unborn child from sorcery. These figures, too, have reproductions of decorative scars.

Many of the decorative patterns embody deep meanings. For instance circles and spirals symbolize the sun and moon, standing for hope and vitality. A double wavy line signifies the human heart as the driving force of human life and the growth of the child in the womb. Scars near the navel, on the other hand, show the close relationship to the ancestors and the continuity of the generations.

◄ The scarifications of Nuba men are much less spectacular than the ornamental scars of the Luluwa women. They show the illnesses overcome and – as a distinction – extraordinary personal achievements.

► The head and neck of this Luluwa motherhood figure are covered with a variety of decorative scars, denoting healthy and flawless skin and the particular psychological and physical qualities of the wearer.

Painted bodies, painted walls: living art forms among the Loma

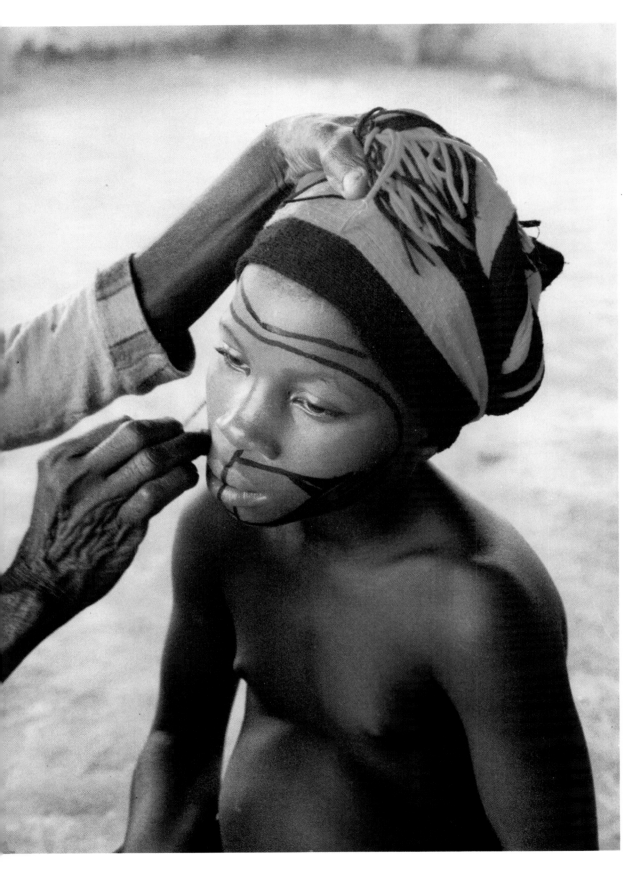

In many African societies body-painting is dying out or has become a tourist attraction. For the Loma in Guinea, however, the ancient art is still very much alive, although painting was banned during Sekou Touré's dictatorship. It is only the women who paint their bodies; this is known as *podai*. Until a few years ago it was only done at the time of the girls' initiation ceremony, but more recently women have begun to apply some of the patterns in permanent form to their house walls as well. The body artists of the Loma are an impressive reminder that not only are the old traditions not dying out in Africa, they are actually being creatively developed, often generating fascinating new artistic forms.

◄ Girls in the bush camps are painted in private by especially gifted women. The paints may be applied in public only after the feast that ends the rites of passage is over. The line across the lips signifies that the girls have to remain silent during the rites of passage until the dancing is over.

During the initiation rites the girls live in bush camps outside their settlements. A day or two before they return, the women appointed by the families of the initiands go to the Sacred Grove to paint the bodies of the novices. A gifted painter can earn a great deal of money on such occasions, because every family is anxious to have its daughter painted by the best and most creative artists. Only black is used the body-painting – the pigment being made of charcoal and oil from the nuts of the *podai* tree – although sometimes a few white lines in kaolin are also added.

The clear lines and areas of solid colour, in combinations often reminiscent of stylized plants, are characteristic of Loma painting. An important feature is the 'lip-closing line', running from under the nose across the mouth to the chin. Since the colours fade after a short time, they are freshly painted every two or three days.

The other women have their bodies painted for the ceremony as well as the initiands. Even babies and small children are painted for the occasion. After the ceremony the newly initiated girls visit their relatives and friends in the neighbouring villages.

▶ Not only are the Loma's body-paintings extraordinarily aesthetic, they also mark the change from the natural state to the realm of culture. When the colours fade after the transition ceremonies are over, the girls are regarded as adult and marriageable women. This girl was painted by Gaou Beayogui, one of the best Loma artists.

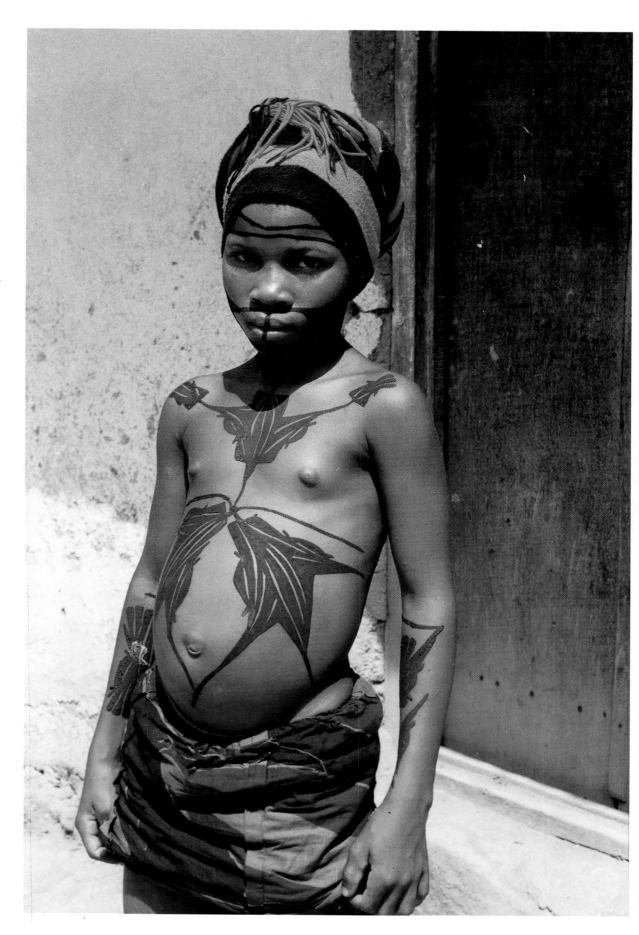

Africa

A young Samburu man in warrior's array.

1. Ashanti
2. Bakuba
3. Bambara
4. Batetela
5. Berber
6. Biombo
7. Bumi
8. Dinka
9. Fingo
10. Ga'anda
11. Hemba
12. Kaleri
13. Karo
14. Kikuyu
15. Kuyu
16. Lobi
17. Loma
18. Luluwa
19. Masai
20. Mangbetu
21. Mbaye
22. Mursi
23. N'Dengese
24. Nkanu
25. Nuba
26. Punu
27. Samburu
28. Shilluk
29. Songye
30. Surma
31. Tabwa
32. Turkana
33. Woodabe
34. Xhosa
35. Yaka
36. Yoruba

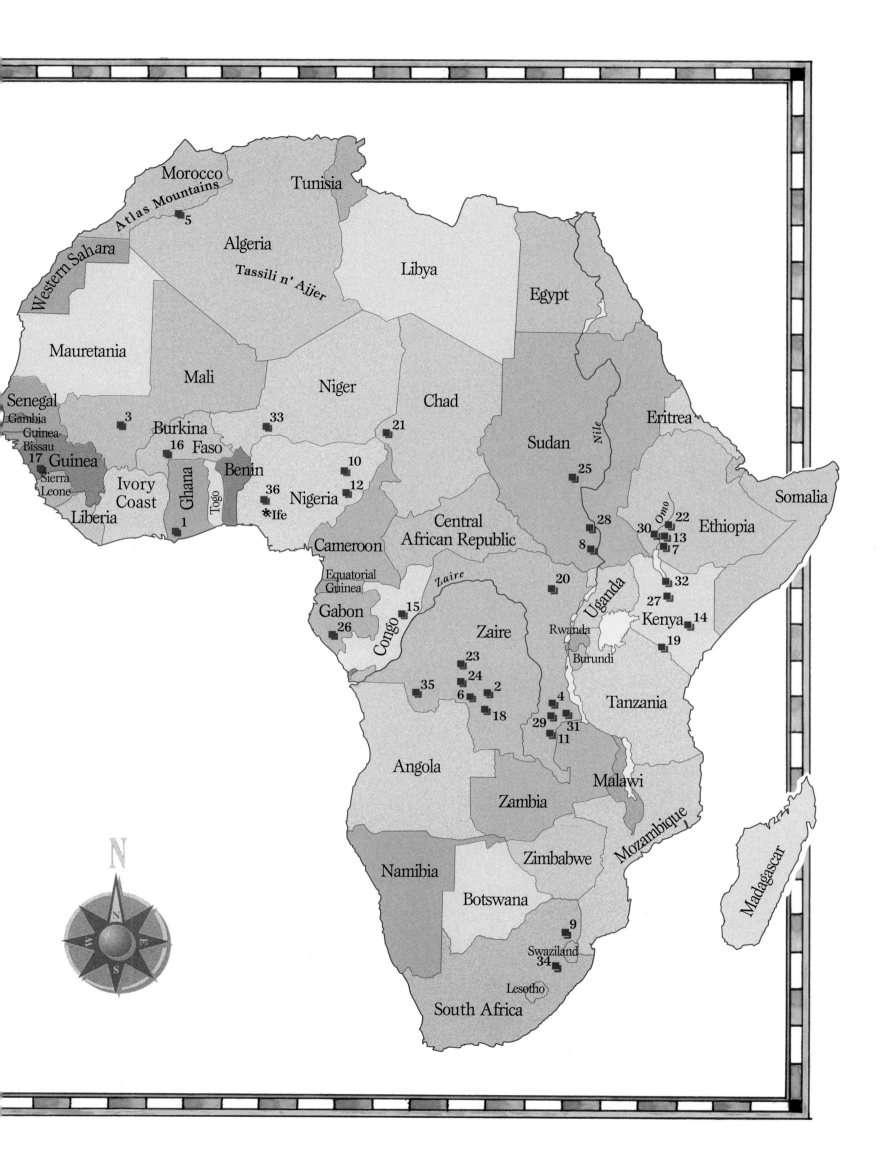

Morocco

Tunisia

Atlas Mountains

5

Western Sahara

Algeria

Libya

Egypt

Mauretania

Mali

Niger

Chad

Sudan

Eritrea

Nile

Senegal

3

33

21

Somalia

Gambia

Burkina

Guinea-Bissau

16

Faso

Benin

10

25

Omo

22

17

Guinea

12

28

30

13

Ethiopia

Sierra Leone

Ivory Coast

Ghana

Togo

36

Nigeria

7

Central African Republic

8

Liberia

1

✳Ife

Cameroon

32

Equatorial Guinea

Zaire

20

Uganda

27

14

Gabon

15

Kenya

26

Congo

Rwanda

19

23

Burundi

35

24

2

Tanzania

6

18

4

29

31

Malawi

11

Angola

Zambia

Mozambique

Madagascar

Namibia

Zimbabwe

Botswana

9

Swaziland

34

Lesotho

South Africa

N

A world of symbols:
India, Nepal, Indonesia

Indian culture is imbued with symbolism. Colours, numbers and artificial shapes or shapes derived from nature are used as symbols for religious or everyday purposes and not only on the skin.

Facial make-up plays an important role in India. For instance, mothers often put lampblack around their babies' eyes to protect them against the Evil Eye. But colours are also indicative of a person's social status. In many places women dye their hair partings red to show they are married. Brides are particularly beautifully decorated, their skin lightened with rice water and rice powder to make it gleam like the moon. Their faces are carefully made up with red and black, and the soles of their feet and palms are dyed red with henna. Complicated patterns are drawn on the backs of their hands and the tops of their feet, also with henna.

The painted or tattooed decorations, worn mostly in the rural areas and by the non-Hindu indigenous population, are also very important. The face is decorated with dots, stripes, moon shapes, flower, leaf and tendril patterns, and the women especially, but also the men, decorate their hands, arms, feet and lower legs with tattoos and artistic patterns.

Those who have devoted their lives to religion, in particular, have marks painted on (or, less commonly nowadays, burned into) their foreheads, in the hope of securing the blessing of the god they worship. The clothing and body markings of the ascetics are full of deep symbolic significance. Red, orange, yellow, ochre and pink are the colours of fire, the rising sun, blood, the earth. They are the colours preferred by adherents of Shivaism and to some extent also Vishnuism. Even animals sometimes have symbolic patterns on their skins. Working elephants and bulls are decorated in this way for particular feast days, but even cows and dogs sometimes have a red dot on their foreheads.

The make-up used in the Indian dance theatre has a different function. Like a mask, it denotes the character of the figure represented. Its colours are purely symbolic, and they have no connection with natural body colours. Nor have the colours used to depict gods in pictures. The god Rama for instance – victor over the demon king Ravana – is often depicted in blue, and Vishnu – the destroyer of all enemies – in black. The colours that the Hindus associate with the four social strata, or *varna* (from the Sanskrit *varna*, 'colour') are also not natural skin shades.

> During these cermony's
> Actos would Act
> -Storytelos would tell stoys
> - Poets would share
> their peotry.

> ► Every year the old gods return to a coastal strip in south-west India, not far from Bangalore. The feast of Teyyam is a religious service, harvest festival, popular theatre and settlement of accounts with the authorities. Experienced and practised actors from the lower castes of rural society put on fantastic masks and exercise divine power for a couple of days and nights. It takes three hours to make up a Teyyam actor's face with plant colouring. (1985)

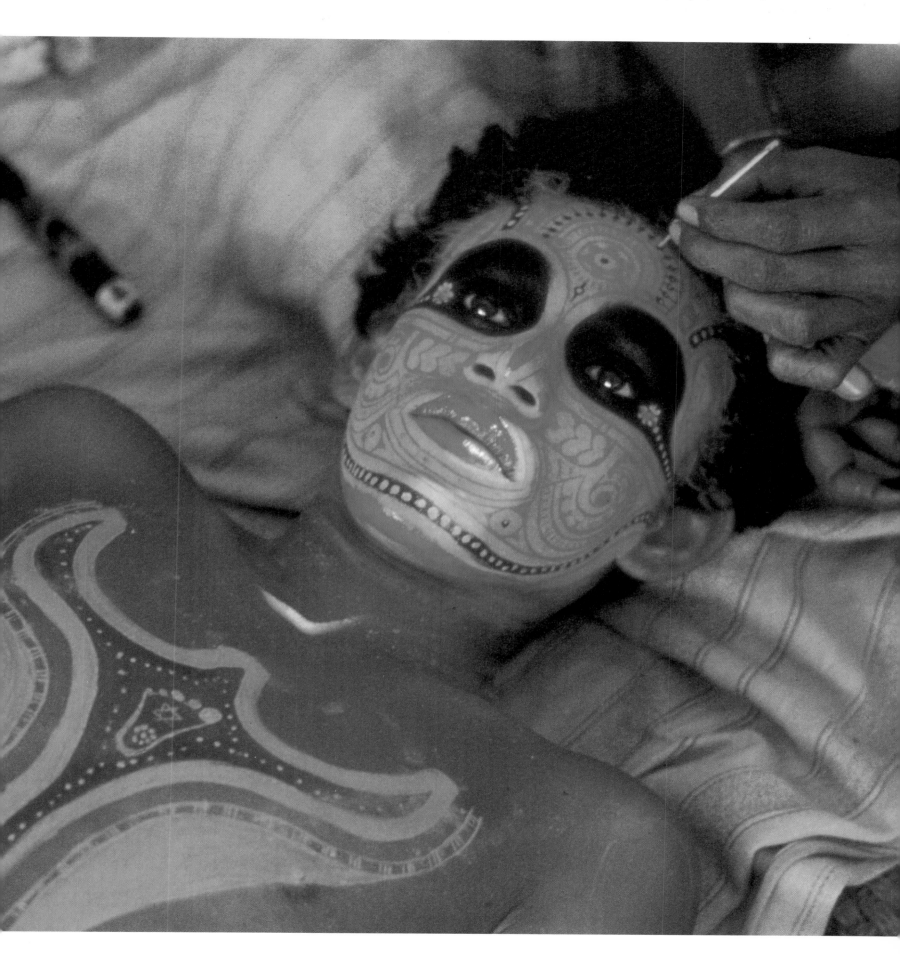

Marks on the forehead

Hindus regard the forehead, which is not contaminated by any excretions, as an especially pure part of the body, and many of them wear a coloured mark there. The women usually have a red dot, which is at the same time a sign of blessing and a decoration. They put it on in the morning, or it is printed on when they go to the temple. It can also be elaborated according to local tradition or the promptings of fashion.

Men have a large number of highly specific forehead markings, showing their religious beliefs. Each religious community has its own marking, the individual components of which are highly significant. Members of the various Hindu religious communities and – particularly on religious occasions – their lay followers are identifiable by these symbols. They are not caste marks denoting social class, since many religious communities do not distinguish between castes.

Nowadays the women mainly use artificial colouring powder from the bazaar for the red marks on their foreheads; previously they used a powder made from the glandular hairs of the kamala tree or a paste from the heartwood of the red sandalwood tree. Red religious markings are, however, still painted on with red sandalwood paste, yellow with a substance from the bark of another sandalwood tree or the rhizome of the turmeric plant. A white paste is mixed from chalk and rice powder (ascetics, though, often use white earth from the banks of the Ganges or ash), and lampblack or charcoal are used for black pigments.

▲ Followers of Shiva usually have three horizontal lines drawn across their foreheads. A crescent moon, probably derived from a bull's horns, and the 'third eye of knowledge' also occur frequently.

▲ This young woman from Rajasthan does not realize the full significance of her discreet make-up. She only knows that the red dot on her forehead and the black marks – which can be either tattooed or painted – protect her from evil. The precious jewellery is 'woman's property'.

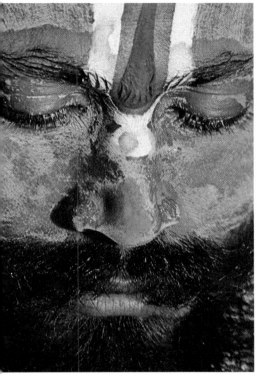

◄ Many followers of Vishnuism have a U-shaped mark, a reference to Vishnu's footprint. The stripe between stands for Lakshmi, Vishnu's wife.

▲ The characteristic face-painting on this young pilgrim in the south Indian state of Tamil Nadu identifies him as a follower of Shivaism. Photographed near Madurai, 1995.

Striving for perfection

Every year crowds of people from
all walks of life set out to cleanse
themselves from sin by bathing in
rivers at one of the numerous places of
pilgrimage. With them go thousands
of men, and even a few women, who
have devoted themselves to the
religious life. Most belong to a
religious community, worshipping
Vishnu or Shiva (the two main Hindu
gods) or following a doctrine in which
the female energy principle *shakti* is
supreme. They are attached to a
temple, live as hermits or move
constantly from one place to another,
and many of them go around naked
or wear orange cloths. Depending on
their beliefs they meditate, engage in
ascetic practices, celebrate orgiastic
rituals, give advice or live off alms.
Some are confidence-tricksters or
vagrants, but many believe that they
can transcend the human, achieve
superhuman strength or attain a
divine or redemptive state. They wear
the sign of their religion on their
foreheads and often other symbols
on their bodies. Worshippers of the
destroyer and creator Shiva, in
particular, often model themselves
on the picture of their god and cover
their bodies with ash from a place of
worship. Whilst adherents of other
faiths – especially those who seek
spiritual strength through yoga –
shave their heads, those of an ecstatic
tendency wear it piled up or loose and
dressed with cows' urine and ashes.

● (Left): Whether gods come down to
earth as men or whether men can attain
godliness through asceticism has been the
subject of debate amongst Hindus for
years. This holy man, sitting on his
throne in the meditation position, is a
kind of god to his followers. (Right): A
startling example of ascetic practice.

Mehndi beautifies brides

The leaves and stems of the henna plant, *mehndi*, produce a reddish-yellow colour well-known as a hair dye. Many Indian women use it to decorate their hands and feet, especially at weddings.

▲ In the villages of Rajasthan and Gujarat, brides have always been decorated with *mehndi*. But this form of decoration is also popular today in urban circles interested in arts and crafts. Henna painting goes well with the red wedding sari and the elaborate jewellery worn on the arms.

They make a paste by mixing the sap with slaked lime and draw delicate patterns with it. Nowadays these are merely decorative, although it used to be believed that they were magic and brought good luck.

▲ Noblewoman at her toilet, with four girls assisting. Mogul empire, early seventeenth century.

▲ Many *mehndi* paintings are reminiscent of fabric designs from the appropriate area. Unfortunately, like many of the works of art that women create, they do not last long.

Pictures of gods

Although Indian gods are usually depicted in pictures in the form of human figures, they can be a completely different colour. This results from the tendency in Indian thought to list, classify and interpret, which has encouraged the growth of elaborate symbolism. According to various theories, colours are associated with specific numbers, notes tunes, moods, points of the compass, planets, bodily functions and – not least because of their relationship with these things – gods. A great many gods are nearly always shown with blue skins, no doubt because the colour blue has both spiritual and erotic associations in India, but (particularly in the contexts of meditation, medicine and magic) the same god can appear in a variety of colours. For instance, in connection with daily observance Vishnu, the preserver, is usually painted blue; but in order to entice a person with magic, people meditate on a white-skinned Vishnu, and on an aggressive red Vishnu to force someone to their knees.

Decoration puts the finishing touches to the picture that people have of a god in India. Just as with human beings, this can be in the form of precious stones, gold and silver jewellery and make-up and powder. Consequently, pictures show gods, too, with coloured decoration painted on their bodies.

◄ Shiva, waited on attentively by his wife. In this picture the god is shown heavily stylized in ash blue. Jewellery, make-up and painted marks enhance his beauty. *Verre églomisé* painting from Rajasthan.

▲ Hanuman, the monkey general, carrying Rama and Lakshmana in the fight against the demon Ravana. Hanuman is an aggressive red; Rama, as a manifestation of Vishnu, blue; Lakshmana light-skinned like a human. All three are elaborately decorated. *Verre églomisé* painting from Rajasthan.

▶ Vishnu with his retinue of demigods and demons. The greenish-blue colouring of their bodies is a reminder that Vishnu is the god of water, air and space. Both the god and his retinue have marks on their foreheads. *Verre églomisé* painting from Rajasthan.

Children as deities

In India and the neighbouring Himalayan countries many of the gods worshipped ultimately represent various aspects of a mother deity. Among them are the 'living goddesses', little girls treated as goddesses until they reach puberty. The 'living goddesses' of Nepal, the *kumaris*, are particularly famous. The most important is based in Kathmandu, in a building near the royal palace that is richly decorated with carvings. She is an embodiment of the mother goddess Taleju – the royal family's powerful tutelary goddess – who is also identified with Durga, the wife of the god Shiva.

About every ten years the *kumari* of Kathmandu is sought out from among the three- to four-year-old daughters of high-ranking Buddhist families, who must be from the Newar community. The girl must be physically perfect and must undergo a test of courage in the form of an exacting ritual. She then lives in her palace, looked after by her mother and the priests. On certain feast days the *kumari* is led through the streets of the city in a procession of carriages, accompanied by two boys representing the gods Ganesha and Bairava. One of her duties is to mark a red dot on the king's forehead every year and so bless him for his new term of office. The *kumari* is believed to have sooth-saying powers, and the king also consults her on important decisions.

◄ The 'living goddess' of Kathmandu – regally decked with jewels, with white-powdered face and the 'third eye' in the red background on her forehead – shows herself to her admirers on certain feast days. She is the tutelary goddess of the Nepalese royal household.

▲ These boys dressed up as gods help to support their clan. Many Hindus believe that they will acquire merit if they give alms to the two of them, whom they recognize as Vishnu (left) and Shiva (right) from the marks on their foreheads and other attributes.

▶ The *Chabahi kumari* at a prayer ceremony. Previously homage was paid to her in a district of Kathmandu, now she is adored by members of her own *bahi*, a monastery. She has to make herself available whenever believers need to worship her.

Symbolic make-up of the kathakali dance theatre

In Kerala, one of the most fertile regions of South India, the art of dance has reached its apogee with the kathakali. This pantomime dance theatre, with song and instrumental accompaniment, performs mythological stories, *katha*. It originated in the seventeenth century from experiments with religious and court dances – which in turn were based on the old tribal dances, the sword dances of the warrior class and on classical Indian dance, with its rich language of gestures, recounting the Hindu myths. Kathakali is secular dance theatre in the sense that it has no connection with temple worship, but the content, taken from Hindu literature, and the rituals at the beginning and end of performances give it a religious veneer. Every performance is basically a ritual for the rebirth of the community.

In kathakali the dancers wear painted make-up, which does not impede their breathing and mimicry, rather than wooden masks. The make-up bears no relation to natural skin colours but is symbolic and is meant to express the ruling passions and emotions of the characters. Green stands for good, red for anger, and black for what is repellent. Applying the make-up is a long, slow process that is carried out by experts while the dancer relaxes, gradually transforming himself into the strongly characterized figure that he will play.

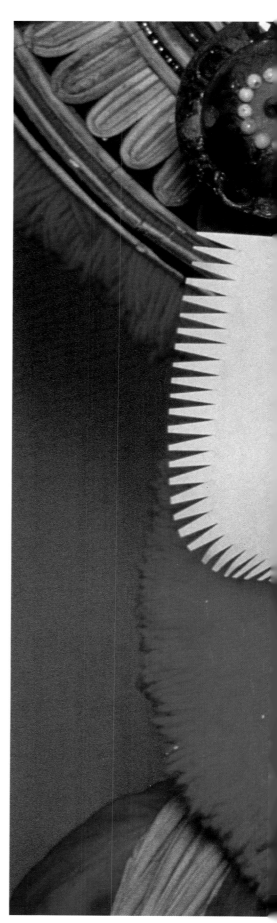

● The make-up of the Kathakali dancers is so complicated that it has to be applied by experts. This often takes several hours. The white eyeballs are reddened by rubbing in plant seeds, so that the movement of the eyes is clearly visible.

The Gond: pictures of the sun and moon

Gondwana (country of the Gond) is the name that the five million or so Gond give to the part of central India where they are settled. Among their number are two closely related groups, the Muria and Maria from Bastar.

The Muria, in particular, are famous far beyond their borders for a unique social institution: the *ghotul*. In these youth houses, to which only the youths or (in the case of the Muria) the boys and girls of a village belong, the young people spend their nights until they marry. The *ghotul* prepare them for marriage and provide a fascinating example of an independent community of children and young people in a society. Their members run their own affairs and, subject to certain conventions, have virtually complete sexual freedom but are instructed in the religion of their society. The *ghotul* are schools of their society and help the young people on their road to adulthood and its responsibilities.

At the onset of puberty, both Muria and Maria girls normally have their bodies tattooed by their mothers with sharp iron needles and black powdered charcoal. The Maria also decorate their faces with elaborate patterns.

◄ The face of this young Maria is decorated with the traditional tattoo patterns. A circle on the forehead symbolizes the full moon, a crescent the half moon; a circle with a dot in the middle is the sign of the sun.

● (Right): A devout Hindu woman on a pilgrimage to the sacred Ganges has had the word 'Rama' written across her face and sari, showing her veneration of the divine hero who symbolizes the ideal man. Symbols can only be understood in their cultural context; the meaning of the astonishingly similar pattern (left) on this ancestor figure from the Cook Islands is not known.

● The traditional patterns – dots and symbols – all have special names. They are applied to arms and legs in decorative longitudinal and diagonal rows.

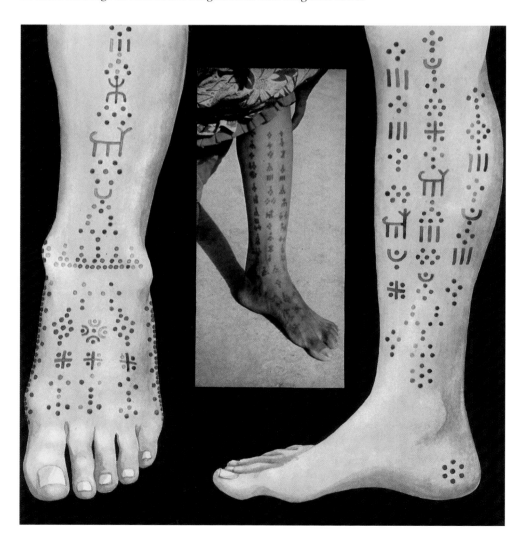

The art of tattooing in Kutch

In the district of Kutch on India's north-west coast, tattooing is an art practised and handed down by the women. The traditional patterns are used as a woman's personal adornment and are an external sign of prosperity – even if it is only minimal. Put on at various stages of life, but especially soon after marriage, the decorations also document the life of an adult woman, whose face is not generally seen as 'humanly beautiful' until it has been tattooed.

In some regions there is still in all the larger villages a woman who knows how to prick out the traditional patterns and prepare the essences used. The black pigment is made by mixing lampblack with tannin extracted from the bark of the kino tree or with milk or urine; tannin decocted from the bark of the bio tree makes bright green patterns. The only tool the tattooists use is a single needle, and only the visible parts of the body are decorated: the face, neck, the upper part of the breasts, arms, hands and feet.

In some areas of Kutch women with particular occupations – such as herdswomen, comb-makers or travelling smiths – also have small tattooed caste marks. The men are tattooed far less often than the women: generally only at annual markets, for fun or to show off. They choose pictures of animals (especially the dromedary, the Kutch herdsman's favourite animal) or symbolic representations of religious myths.

Dots and figurative symbols

▲ The patterns on this woman's neck are arranged in a horizontal line, like ornamental chains. In the village of Modsar women ask their husband's permission if they want to be tattooed.

The traditional patterns are applied singly or in rows, depending on the part of the body. The face is decorated just with a few individual dots, perhaps on the forehead, chin and cheeks, or on the top lip and next to the eyes. The palms of the hands – which are particularly sensitive to pain – are heavily tattooed, and the young girls and women willingly endure the pain in order to be beautiful. Normally it is two to three days before the pain eases and the swelling goes down.

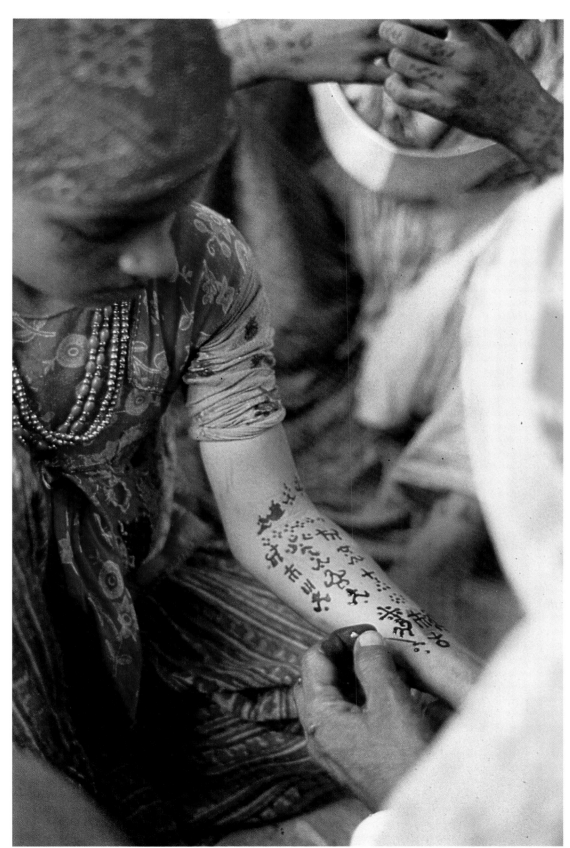

▲ Before decorations are tattooed into the skin, with laborious precision, they are drawn on with Indian ink – here on the forearm of a young woman. All photos on this and previous page date from 1972.

Last representatives of an ancient culture: the Andamanese

In the islands of the Andaman chain in the Gulf of Bengal, which has belonged to India since 1950, only a few hundred of the indigenous inhabitants remain on the habitable islands. They are the descendants of a historic ethnic group that still survives in a few parts of South-East Asia. Until the end of the eighteenth century they lived in complete isolation and had their own languages, unrelated to other linguistic groups. Their economy – hunting, fishing and gathering – was ideally suited to the tropical rain forests where they lived.

However, the islands have been systematically colonized since the nineteenth century. New settlements were established, and large areas of the rain forest cleared; the indigenous population fell prey to hitherto unknown diseases and many died. Sadly, the few surviving Andamanese – the Onge, Jarawa and Sentinelese – may well soon suffer the same fate as the Great Andamanese, whose culture has already disappeared.

Body and face-painting – varying from group to group – still plays an important role (only among the Great Andamanese was tattooing customary). Applied for both decorative and talismanic purposes, it can also have ritual significance, for instance in times of mourning.

◄ The paint was thickly spread on this child's face and the pattern then scratched on with fingertips or small sticks.

► Face-painting is an essential part of daily body care, and also an effective protection against insects (all illustrations on this and next page show Onge).

Colour of life, colour of light

Three basic materials are available to the Andamanese: simple grey clay, known as *odu*, the particularly valuable rare white argillaceous clay, *tol*, and ochre. The last, mixed with animal and vegetable fats, produces red colouring.

Only painted bodies are considered strong, healthy and beautiful; the unpainted body, on the other hand, is seen as vulnerable to various diseases and dangers. Red, the colour of blood and fire, often stands for warmth, energy, spiritual and physical activity, vitality, strength and excitement. The people therefore see red ochre, in particular, as medicinal and apply it with honey when ill or take it internally. Even newborn babies are rubbed with light clay and red ochre immediately after birth, and sometimes the skulls of the dead are painted red. Well-being is associated with fine weather, light and light colours. Since *tol* is the lightest colour known, it is used as a visible expression of a positive state.

● The different groups distinguish themselves from each other by means of their distinctive paint patterns, which all group members may wear. For the most part the painting of the face is stressed, its linear pattern being executed with particular care.

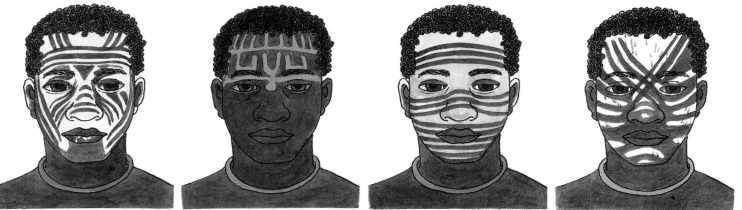

● Often the women of the group are the make-up artists, or else men and women paint each other. Special attention is paid to the elegance and clarity of the lines. Either the whole body is patterned, apart from the face and hands, or central parts of the body, such as the face and chest, are decorated. Sometimes faces are also made-up in unbroken areas of colour, as with this woman drinking from a nautilus shell (right). The painting often also emphasizes family relationships and stresses the unity of the family through its similarities (above).

Mentawai: beauty is the souls' delight

For the inhabitants of Mentawai, an archipelago in the far west of Indonesia, everything that exists has a soul: humans, animals, plants, objects, even a rainbow or a cloudless sky. Both human souls and those of any other phenomena well-disposed towards humanity rejoice at the beautiful aspects of life: festivals, dances, artistic carvings, jewellery, flowers, good food. But if life becomes too monotonous the souls go to the settlements of the dead, and humankind must die.

The striving for beauty – and the goodwill of the souls – therefore governs life. Except at times of mourning, men and women always wear decoration. They are proud of their long, black hair, but they remove their body hair, apart from the eyebrows. The purpose of tattooing – like the sharpening of the incisor teeth at puberty – is to lend the body 'dignity', because a person's soul would not feel at home in a body that was not artistically 'completed' with fine drawings. The face-painting, known as *gobbiat*, is worn mainly for celebrations, to supplement the tattooed lines that cover men's and women's bodies.

◄ A village group from Siberut, where the old forms of decoration survived best.

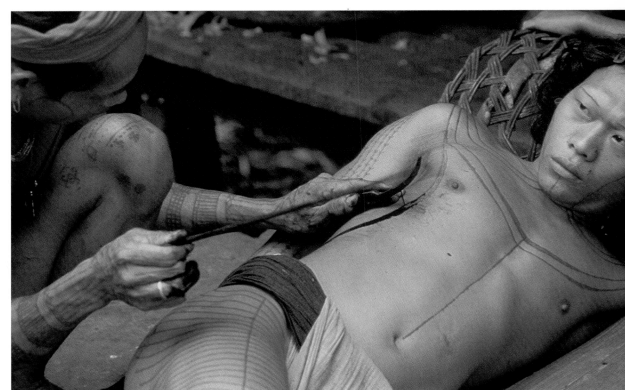

▲ The tattooing instruments are a wooden stick and a horn-handled brass needle on which the colour is spread. The pattern is applied along pre-drawn lines marked on the skin.

Male and female decoration

Tattooing, *titi*, does not begin until the body is fully grown, so that the lines do not lose their shape. It can be done by any adult male in the group, although he must show proof of special skill. Tattooing is very painful, and the patterns are therefore applied in several stages over a period of some years. The tattooing fluid consists of a mixture of lampblack (it used to be a tree resin, *muno*) and sugar-cane juice. The patterns vary from one part of the archipelago to another, and there are also major differences between the male and female decoration. However both sexes have a beautiful spiral drawing on their hands and 'cuffs' and 'leggings' on their forearms and thighs. The main decoration for men is the half-moon-shaped 'pectoral', with curves running up from its centre to the cheeks, a big curve sweeping over the flanks and horizontal lines on the thighs. Successful head-hunters used to be allowed to tattoo themselves with special marks: a toad, as a symbol for a man, on the stomach and spirals on the forehead and shoulders.

After Indonesian independence in 1954 the Mentawai's traditional religion, tattooing and tooth-sharpening were banned by the government. Only on the island of Siberut were many of the old traditions allowed to survive.

◄ A medicine-man applying face-paint. The black colouring, a mixture of sugar-cane juice and soot, is dotted or stroked on the forehead, the end of the nose, cheeks and chin; sometimes it is also contrasted with a yellow paint made from turmeric.

► This girl with a bamboo flute has the female tattoo pattern: a star radiating out from the shoulders, across the chest and back, and up to the chin.

India · Nepal · Indonesia

The Kattalati-huntress of the kathakali theatre.

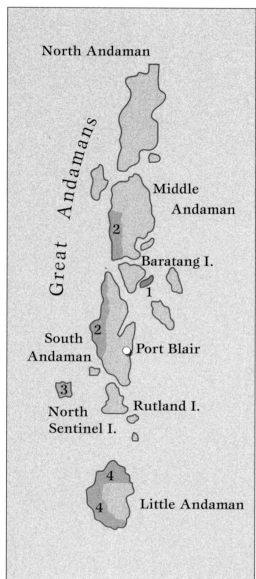

North Andaman

Great Andamans

Middle Andaman

Baratang I.

1

2

South Andaman

2

Port Blair

3

North Sentinel I.

Rutland I.

4

4

Little Andaman

Andamanese
1 Great Andamanese
2 Jarawa
3 Sentinelese
4 Onge

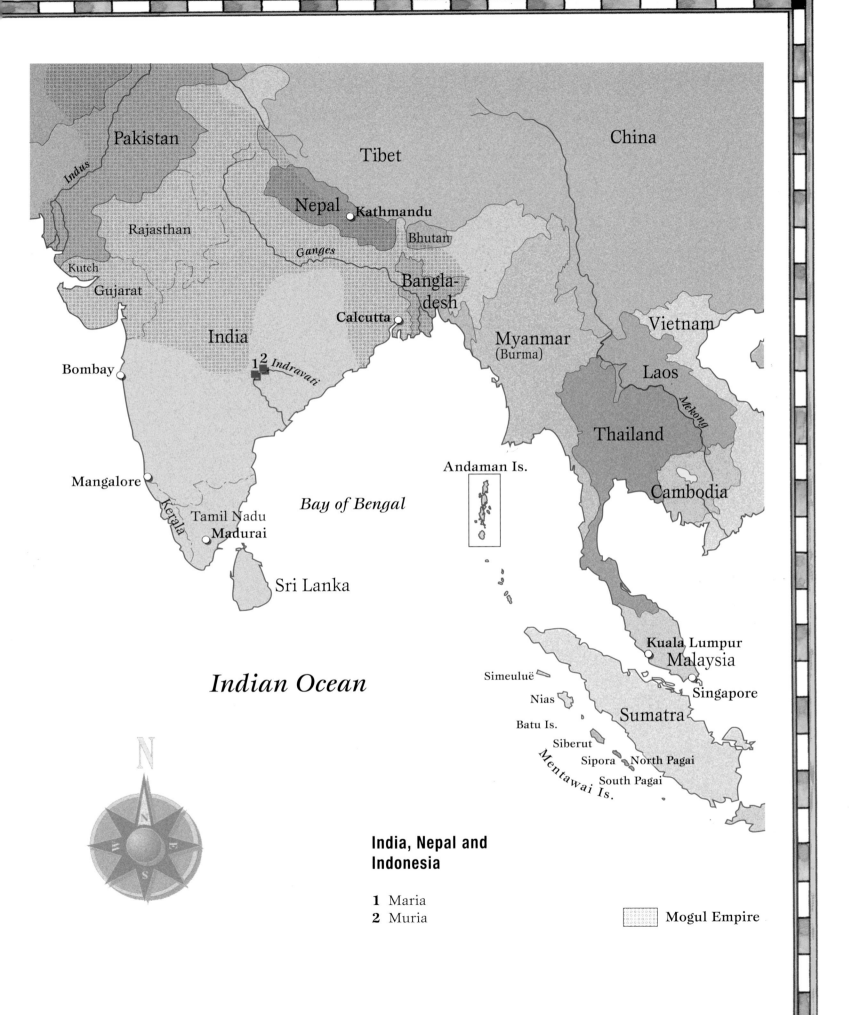

Pakistan

Indus

Tibet

China

Rajasthan

Nepal ○ Kathmandu

Bhutan

Ganges

Kutch

Gujarat

Bangla-
desh

Vietnam

India

Calcutta ○

Myanmar
(Burma)

Bombay ○

1 2 *Indravati*

Laos

Mekong

Mangalore ○

Kerala

Thailand

Tamil Nadu
Madurai

Andaman Is.

Cambodia

Sri Lanka

Bay of Bengal

Indian Ocean

Kuala Lumpur ○
Malaysia

Simeuluë

○ Singapore

Nias

Sumatra

Batu Is.

Siberut

Sipora ◦ North Pagai

Mentawai Is.

South Pagai

N

**India, Nepal and
Indonesia**

1 Maria
2 Muria

Mogul Empire

The 'painted face' of China: Peking Opera make-up

The history of the Peking Opera goes back to the pantomime dances associated with the exorcism of demons, religious worship and the veneration of ancestors as long ago as the third millennium BC. In the period of the Han emperors (206 BC–AD 220) a secular entertainment for the emperor's court developed from the forms of religious worship. Dancing and singing groups were joined by story-tellers, jugglers, magicians and acrobats, thus bringing together the essential elements of present-day Chinese lyrical drama. Chinese annals of the tenth century AD also refer specifically to the 'painted face', which must certainly have been exercising a magic spell at religious festivals for many years before that. Painted make-up is still a fundamental component of mimic expression at the Peking Opera today.

In its present form the Peking Opera has only developed over the last two hundred years. It blends all forms of representative art into a fascinating theatrical panorama; it is at once opera and drama, ballet and pantomime, acrobatic circus show and heroic epic, comedy and melodrama. The faces of the actors, transformed into fantastic sculptures, depict heroes and villains, gods and spirits, and symbolize brutality and feminine gentleness. The audience are trans-ported into a colourful dream world that takes them away from their everyday cares. On the stage the spectators see the of feats and adventures of the historic heroes, some still venerated as gods, and the exploits of their mythical helpers unfolding anew before their eyes.

● The narrow oval face with lines sweeping out diagonally around the almond eyes is the ideal of beauty for gentle theatrical femininity, which can conquer even tyrants. Actresses, or actors in a female role (as recently as the nineteenth century it was considered improper for men and women to appear on stage together), apply the 'colour of the peony' to the cheeks and eyes on a pale pink background. The chin, nose and forehead are left light, making the face look narrower.

▲ Dance and pantomime are essential components of the Peking Opera.

▲ The make-up of the divine dragon king, who leads the army of the gods against the monkey kingdom; it includes gold, the symbol of supernatural beings. The face-paint shines on stage; oil or egg-white is usually mixed with it, making the face more lively and expressive.

The actor as Theatre

In the Chinese lyrical drama the music and action are not the predominant elements – the actors themselves are the theatre. It is in the elegance of their stylized movements on the empty stage, the subtle symbolism of the character make-up, the perfect pantomime that the magic of the Peking Opera resides. Even the movements of the long silk sleeves express a wide variety of moods. Every position of the foot, every gesture is part of an overall composition of movement based on strict rules, with accents added by whirling, dance-like sword-fights and acrobatic interludes.

The Opera makes extraordinary and lifelong demands on the actors, who begin lessons and physical training while they are still children. The up-and-coming young actors are known as 'students of the pear orchard' – after China's first theatre school, set up by the T'ang emperor Xuan Zong (AD 712–756), a lover of the arts, in the pear orchard of his palace. Hundreds of talented young men were trained as dancers, singers and musicians under a strict regime. In a separate school, 'the garden of the eternal spring', beautiful young girls received their artistic training under the direct supervision of the emperor, learning also how to apply the make-up that emphasizes the expressions of the female mimes.

▲ The actor playing the dragon king at the Peking Opera, putting on his wig, which is decorated with red cords. (Peking, 1951)

▼ On the Chinese stage most of the colours are symbolic, including those used for the make-up. A red face signifies a faithful, honest and steadfast character: (1) The red face of the god of war. Black symbolizes an impetuous person, but also a person acting according to the strict law of the state, for example (2) the judge Pchen Chen. (3) Stylized bull make-up. (4) Shattered face. (5) Peach-blossom make-up. (6) General Meng Lian. (7) Crane make-up. (8) Monkey king.

In Chinese mythology the white tiger is the king of the beasts. The imperial colour yellow around the eyes of the make-up scheme denotes his rank. The tiger in the stories can even fend off particularly evil and powerful demons, against which the tutelary spirits that watch over every house are helpless. A colleague is helping the actor playing the white tiger into his costume. Contemporary costumes are more magnificent and colourful than the historical clothing. (Peking, 1952)

Different patterns for different types of character

In the early stages of the Chinese lyrical drama the make-up – unmistakably in the tradition of the religious ceremonies, where it served to ward off evil spirits – was usually black-and-white and fierce-looking. The colour was applied roughly with the fingers. Gradually more colours, from plant and mineral sources, were added until elaborate artistic compositions developed, which then required a brush.

Specific symbolic colours and make-up patterns denote each character type. A predominance of red indicates courage, loyalty and faithfulness – it is the colour for heroes and leaders of armies. Strong black outlines are the sign of impetuous characters. A white face expresses brutality and depravity, while a single white patch across the nose and eyes, extending as far as the cheekbones, denotes the clown and also stands for petty scoundrels, common people and underlings. A blue face stands for cruelty, a yellow face for reticence. Demons and devils have green faces; and those of heavenly beings are outlined in bright yellow, the imperial colour.

► The 'hook' is one of the four main methods of face-painting at the Peking Opera. It is used for all types of face-painting and is the most important technique of linear composition. The designs for actors playing painted mask roles are drawn with great speed and precision, using the 'hook face' method. The paint brush is held still, touching the face; while the outlines of the design are as it were 'hooked out' by a series of separate gliding movements of the head.

▲ The monkey king making one of his characteristic gestures. The repertoire of gestures has to be fully mastered to achieve rich characterization in the Chinese lyrical drama. (Peking, 1972)

◄ The monkey king. The red contours of the make-up scheme are a stylized artistic representation of a monkey's face and at the same time denote cleverness and courage. The monkey king Sun Wu-kung is wearing the yellow gown of the emperor. The king's helmet is ornamented with lavish decoration and slender pheasant feathers. (Peking, 1972)

The monkey king Sun Wu-kung: a popular symbol in Chinese mythology

In the play *Uproar in Heaven* the Peking Opera uses make-up with particular artistic virtuosity. The action centres around a popular symbolic figure in Chinese mythology – the monkey king Sun Wu-kung – who, fighting for a just cause, triumphs even over an army of gods.

Sun feels he has been betrayed in heaven because he has been given a grandiose title but no position. So he provokes the gods: he eats the sacred peach destined for the table of the king of heaven and drinks the precious elixir of life. Then he goes back to his mountains. The outraged dragon king (the dragon is usually an imperial symbol) leads the army of the gods against the monkey kingdom. But Sun, who survives breathtaking sword-fights on stage, beats the gods with his monkey army.

The monkey is popularly seen as a symbol of the simple man who wins an epic victory over the mighty. In the legend the pantheon of gods, with its countless deities responsible for all possible aspects of life on earth, stands as a metaphor for the imperial bureaucratic state. The Chinese, more than any other people, have cast their gods in their own image and have humanized them. And their religion has always been closely linked with philosophy and a very pragmatic outlook.

▶ The actor Li Shao Ch'uan, a famous interpreter of the monkey king role, in his dressing room at a Peking theatre, 1960. The monkey king, the most popular fantasy figure, is the main character in the romance *Journey to the West*, set in the T'ang period, an inexhaustible source of many popular pieces at the Peking Opera.

Red face and black beard:

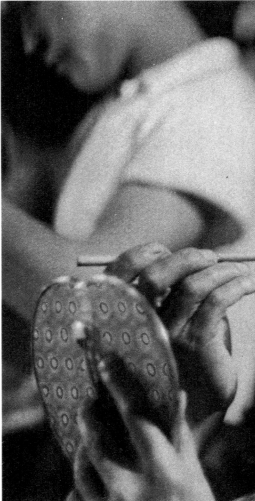

◄ ▲ General Guan Yu with plum-red face
and black beard, putting on his make-up
in his dressing room. (Left): The same
character in a production in Peking,
c. 1954.

The linear design of the make-up
may vary slightly to suit the actor's
features. This leaves scope for
individual artistic conceptions and
the different styles of face-painting
found nowadays in the Peking Opera.
However some basic designs and
colours are traditionally regarded as
appropriate to the characterization of
particular roles. They are essential if
the well-known historic figures are to

General Guan Yu

be recognized at a glance. They include, for instance, the make-up for Guan Yu, the red-faced general of Shu in the Three Kingdoms period (220–280). A literary account of events in this period in the third century AD appears in the long romance *Stories from the Three Kingdoms*, probably dating from the Ming dynasty (1368–1644), used as a basis for the Peking Opera repertoire.

▲ The make-up of the red-faced general Guan Yu, a popular and revered figure in Chinese history, dating from the Three Kingdoms period (AD 220–280). He fought violent battles to reunite the empire under Han rule. Later he was elevated to the rank of a god and venerated as the god of war and also the god of literature. His famous black beard is noticeably longer, thicker and glossier than any of the others on the stage. (Taiwan, 1970)

Japan: painted skin, decorated bodies

The painted face, which since the earliest times has been used by humans as an adornment or to endow themselves with magic powers, matured in Japan into the aesthetic basis of an ideal of beauty valid for centuries. At the same time it developed into an artistic component of mimic expression in the theatre. This cultural legacy, which still survives today, is expressed in the stylized make-up of the geishas and the artistic face-painting of the kabuki actors. Even when Japanese culture first blossomed in the Heian period (794–1185 AD), stereotyped white face make-up was a attribute of beauty for aristocratic women at the imperial court in Kyoto. Their personal radiance was discreetly accentuated by luxurious clothing of silks and brocades whose subtle blending of colours and patterns indicated their high rank.

When the splendour and power of the small aristocracy declined, and Edo (now Tokyo) emerged as the new capital in the seventeenth century, the white face of the nobles became the badge of office of cultivated entertainers – the geishas. They were the 'aristocrats' of the closed entertainment districts that developed at that time and survived until the immediate post-war period; today only a few geisha houses offer their luxury services on the fringes of politics and big business.

As a middle class emerged, the kabuki theatre – still traditional today – developed from roots in the colourful Chinese lyrical drama, while the classical Noh theatre of the Kyoto court aristocracy, which was bound by a strict code of form and gesture, was pushed into the background. In the lavishly produced kabuki scenarios, the artificial face-painting transports the spectator to the magical world of ancient myths and fairy tales.

On the Japanese islands there is also a long tradition of body-painting, tattooing and scarification, which were used for decorative and religious purposes as long ago as the Neolithic Age. The motivation and background of tattooing has changed over the years. For centuries body patterns were a minor reflection of changes in Japanese society. From a badge of rank they developed into the detested mark of social inferiority for those outside society, and later came to denote membership of a particular profession, but increasingly they were used for decoration. In the modern era tattooing became a recognized expression of supreme skill, which flourishes to this day.

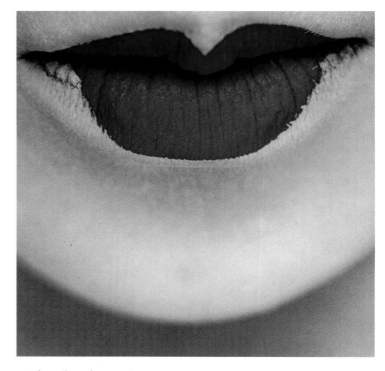

● The white face stylizes the appearance of the geisha, eliminating any individualism and elevating her above the ordinary, like a theatrical character. The fashion for white make-up came from China in the seventh century AD. The Chinese also supplied the women of the imperial court with the white-lead make-up so damaging to the skin; this was used until 1934, when it was banned. The red for the lips, obtained from the flowers of the safflower plant, apparently came from China about 610 AD, at the time of the empress Suiko.

Geishas: precious flowers on the fringe of society

▼ The nape of the neck adorned with white make-up is regarded as particularly alluring and erotic when rising out of the deliberately displayed collar of the kimono, which is a fantasy of delicate colours and patterns.

Like the magic of its temples and gardens, geishas are still part of Japan's romantic image. Their appearance follows traditional rules: with the artificial, piled up hair goes the mask-like white face make-up that in ancient Japan was seen as a sign of nobility and distinguished ladies of high rank from the sunburned members of the lower classes. The small made-up mouth, with red lipstick only on the centre part of the

lips, corresponds to the prevailing ideal of beauty, since a large mouth is considered vulgar. The geishas' exquisite external appearance is accentuated by expensive kimonos. The Japanese masters of the coloured woodcut concentrated entirely on portraying these garments, but paid no particular attention to the body – in contrast to Europe, where it was the naked body that was always a creative challenge to the artist.

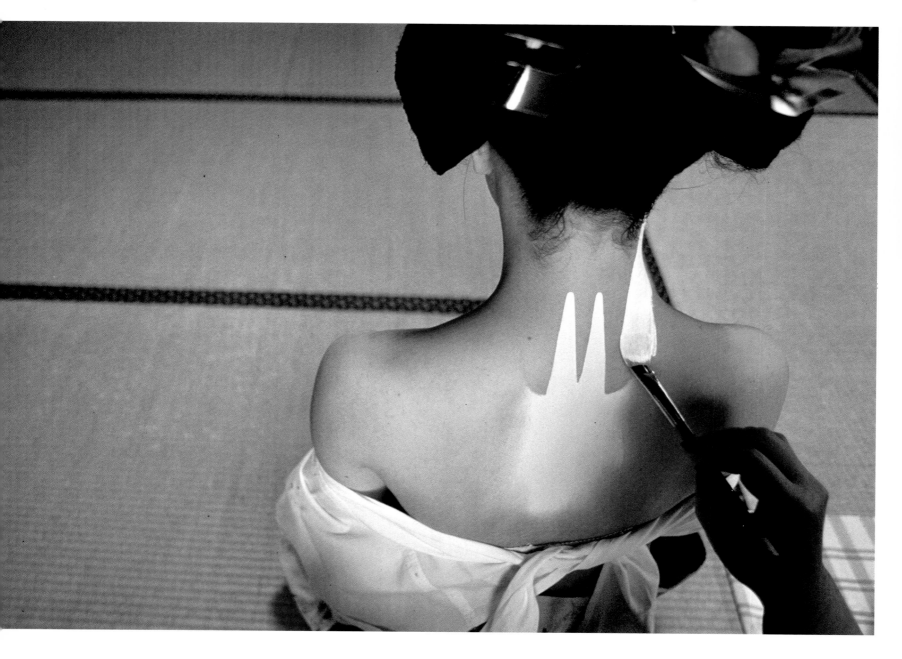

▲ The face of the geisha: its anonymity makes it a screen on which clients can project their wishes.

In Tokyo's entertainment quarters the geishas drive to evening functions in big limousines – taxis would be inappropriate for the fantastic piled up hairstyles, modelled on styles centuries old, and the constricting costumes. As if time had stood still, they then engage in the traditional art of stimulating, witty conversation in the teahouse. Attentively and willingly, they fill *sake* cups, offer lights to smokers and prepare and serve dishes in accordance with strict rules of etiquette. As the evening progresses, interspersed between relaxed conversation, games and serious discussion of business and politics, artistic dances are performed, with every movement highly stylized. These are complemented by *shamisen* accompaniment and old songs with words of flowery frivolity.

The geishas, trained for many years in the musical arts, see themselves as guardians of the old cultural heritage, experts in sophisticated conversation, bound by strict rules of etiquette. Intimate contact is taboo, but that does not exclude privately having a regular customer as their patron.

The history of the geishas goes far back into Japan's past. When power began to slip away from the emperor in Kyoto in the thirteenth and fourteenth centuries, and the samurai warrior castes dominated the scene, cultivated women retreated into the background. Unlike Europe's gallant knights, the *samurai*, bound by the *bushido* code of honour, avoided the sensitive company of cultivated women. The warlords enhanced their exclusive social gatherings with the hired attractions of the *shirabyoshi*, who used to sing at religious festivals in white gowns (*shira* means 'white') and perform religious dances. They now displayed their mimic arts and their gallantry in castles and military quarters like wandering troubadours. From them the model for the classic image of the geisha was derived when, in the early seventeenth century, the shoguns of the Tokugawa clan (who ruled until 1867) seized power, and Edo, now Tokyo, emerged as the new capital.

Kabuki make-up: colours of heroes and villains

In Japan, as in China, the theatre has preserved the painted faces from ancient magic rituals in a stylized artistic form; the medieval theatrical art of kabuki is still flourishing to this day. The popular stage offers an exciting traditional spectacle of great magnificence, conforming to strict rules. These excursions into the world of the old, feudal Japan with its *samurai* and courtesans, gods and spirits, backed by guttural choruses and the rhythms of the drummers, the *shamisen* and *koto* players, last up to eight hours.

Japanese theatre originates in the lyrical drama in neighbouring China – whence the Japanese also took their script, Buddhism, art and craft techniques and, last but not least, the ritual of cultivated social intercourse. However the imported Chinese theatre was developed creatively and evolved into a distinctive Japanese theatre of a high artistic standard. In kabuki dramatic construction is stricter, the stylization of movement and dance more pronounced, the use of colours is more delicate (coloured make-up is less used) and the design more severe. The stage always has to provide beautiful, aesthetic images.

Red and black outlines on a white painted face denote heroism, dedication and honesty. Military leaders and heroes often also have coloured lines on their hands and feet. Blue outlines indicate a bad character, but in different make-up schemes they can represent supernatural phenomena, gods of nature and the spirits of ancestors. The faces of the high-ranking geishas, whose magnificent entrances and processions are the climax of many morality plays, are frozen into white masks. Like all female parts, they are played by men.

Kabuki once had about fifty make-up schemes with fine distinctions of character and role; nowadays there are only about a dozen.

▲ Portrait of an actor with a painted face, on a congratulatory message. Woodcut by Ando Hiroshige (1797–1858), first half of the nineteenth century.

● The red-and-black colouring of the face-paint shows the audience that this is a proud character with a thirst for action. The red lines emphasize the facial muscles, emotively exaggerating the actor's expression.

The female impersonator is the star of kabuki

The female roles played by men, the *onna-gata*, lend a particular charm and sensual appeal to kabuki theatre. They make enormous demands on the actor's powers of mimicry. He would not last a minute if his improvisation was superficial, for the Japanese audience expects a complete mastery of the stylized female movement and body language.

Kabuki was, nonetheless, started by women. In about 1600 the former priestess and temple dancer Okuni, with partners from temple and courtesan circles in Kyoto, put on secular choral and dance displays derived from religious ritual, and these were very well received by audiences. They were joined by male actors. The courtesan flirt was now also delighting teahouse customers with erotic song and dance scenes known as *kabuki* (*ka* means 'song', *bu* 'dance' and *ki* 'artistic'). In 1607 Okuni and her troupe moved to Edo, where they soon provoked such erotic turmoil, with jealous duels and killings, that in 1629 the government banned men and women from appearing on stage together. Commercially-minded organizers then replaced the now very free dancing arts of the courtesans with twelve- to sixteen-year-old boys, which soon led to paedophile scandals. In 1652 the government also banned the boys' kabuki, ending the theatre's direct and crude eroticism. From then on only actors with their foreheads shaved as proof of masculinity could appear; women are still excluded from the kabuki stage to this day.

● The actor Tama Sabuto Bando is famous for his portrayal of female roles. The Bando are a traditional kabuki family.

Body decoration in prehistoric Japan

Archaeological findings suggest that the original inhabitants of Japan were already decorating their bodies in the Neolithic Jomon period (*c.* 10,000–300 BC. As well as simple clay vessels decorated with cord and basket-weave patterns, not at that stage made on a wheel, clay figurines were found with elaborate linear and dot patterns that permit speculation about probable religious body-painting. Female fertility symbols were used in the enactment of religious rituals by the largely coast-dwelling population of hunters, gatherers and fishermen.

Evidence from the later Yayoi period (*c.* 300 BC–AD 300) has provided further information on the practice of prehistoric body-decoration. This was the time when rice-growing was introduced to Japan from China, via Korea, and by then the potter's wheels was in use. Red-painted clay figures about 50–100 cm high, known as *haniwa*, were found in the tumuli in which important chieftains were buried. The meaning of these hollow figures, whose bodies are decorated with orderly and symmetrical patterns, is unclear. According to one – disputed – theory these representations of humans and animals were a substitute for the live human beings and animals that used to accompany a person to his grave and were sacrificed so as to be able to serve their lord in the kingdom of the dead. There are Chinese accounts of Japanese men wearing tattoos of rank in the later Yayoi period.

◄ *Haniwa* (hollow clay figure) from the Tumulus period (AD 250–500) with traces of red face-paint.

The Ainu women of Hokkaido

The origins of the Ainu – only a few of whom now survive on Hokkaido, southern Sakhalin and a few of the Kurile islands – are the subject of great scientific controversy, but both Japanese and Ainu are probably descended from the people of the Jomon civilization. This sedentary people, who at one time also lived on Honshu but were pushed back as the Japanese migrated north, used to be hunters, fishermen and gatherers. The Ainu's traditional religion has almost died out. The only feature that still survives is the worship of bears; but now bear-cult ceremonies are more tourist attractions than religious observances.

Tattooing, whose origins are explained in a number of myths, was practised only by the Ainu women. The significance of the decorations was closely linked to the Ainu religion and also to the social structure: a full tattoo was a characteristic and status symbol of a married woman. The painful operation was carried out by female specialists in several stages over a period of years. Powdered charcoal was rubbed into cuts made in the skin with small sharp knives, giving the young girls a blue-black tattoo tapering to a point at the sides of the mouth. The areas around the eyebrows were also decorated with wavy lines, and the hands and forearms were adorned with a variety of patterns. In the early twentieth century the Ainu women abandoned tattoos, banned by the Japanese government, and instead painted themselves with ink for ceremonial and festive occasions.

▲ Ainu woman with full tattooed mouth, arms and hands, *c.* 1900. Girls were first tattooed with an arc of dots above the mouth in childhood or early youth; thereafter a new line was added each year. On marriage, the pattern was completed by the bridegroom, who executed the pointed extensions.

▲ Ainu woman with distinctive mouth-tattooing, Hokkaido 1953.

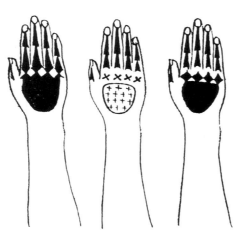

▲ Top: Typical tattoo patterns for the fingers and the backs of the hands.

▲ Bottom: Four different types of mouth-tattooing for women.

From stigma to ornamentation

▲ Two actors with extensive tattoos on their arms and backs, rubbing themselves with towels in the steam bath. Four-colour double-leaf woodcut (1858) by Utagawa Kunisada (1786–1864).

In few other parts of the world has tattooing been developed into such an elaborate art as in Japan, and nowhere else was tattooing for so long woven so closely into the customs of the lower social classes, or so much a means of showing professional solidarity. Its origins are lost in the mists of the pre-modern era.

From the sixth century tattooing was used as a form of punishment. As in China, marks were made on the foreheads or forearms of criminals, to set them aside from the rest of society. In some regions they were tattooed with the character for 'dog', in others with a stripe. At certain times the despised lowest class were also marked

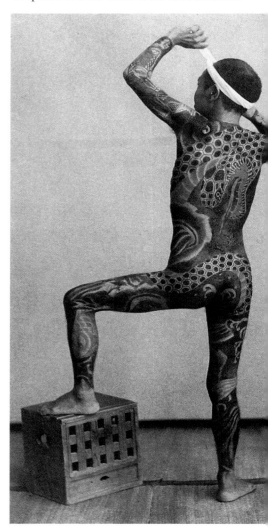

▶ Anonymous photograph of a tattooed Japanese man, *c.* 1880. The complete tattooing of the whole body is called *zenshin-bori*. In the more menial occupations in old Japan full-body tattooing up to the neck was called *sushi-ya-bori*.

▲ Japanese patterns, covering large areas of the body, have been copied all over the world.

out from the rest of society by a tattooed caste mark: the *eta*, who worked as knackers, grave-diggers and labourers at the most menial tasks lived in separate quarters.

Towards the end of the seventeenth century the skin became a medium for indelible vows or religious prayers. The custom of wearing professions of eternal affection on the inside of the arm, and sometimes also more intimately on the thigh, became particularly widespread among the courtesans of the entertainment district. Buddhist monks and devout laymen had prayers written on their backs in calligraphy.

The tattoo had now become a decorative element, but it was still associated with the former labelling of criminals, and therefore frowned upon. When occupational groups in the lowest social classes began to express their solidarity through symbolic body tattoos, the suspicious government in Edo issued several orders banning tattooing, but these had no lasting effect.

A temporary ban was also imposed after the 1868 revolution, when the Shogun government collapsed and the threat of American guns opened up the country, which had been shut off from the world for 250 years, to outside influences. The *gaijin*, the foreigners, were not to be shown a negative picture of Japan. But when in 1881 the heir to the English throne, Prince George, visited Japan with a tattoo of a dragon on his arm, the ban was immediately lifted, and the tattooists enjoyed a new boom.

Nihon irezumi: beauty contest and high art

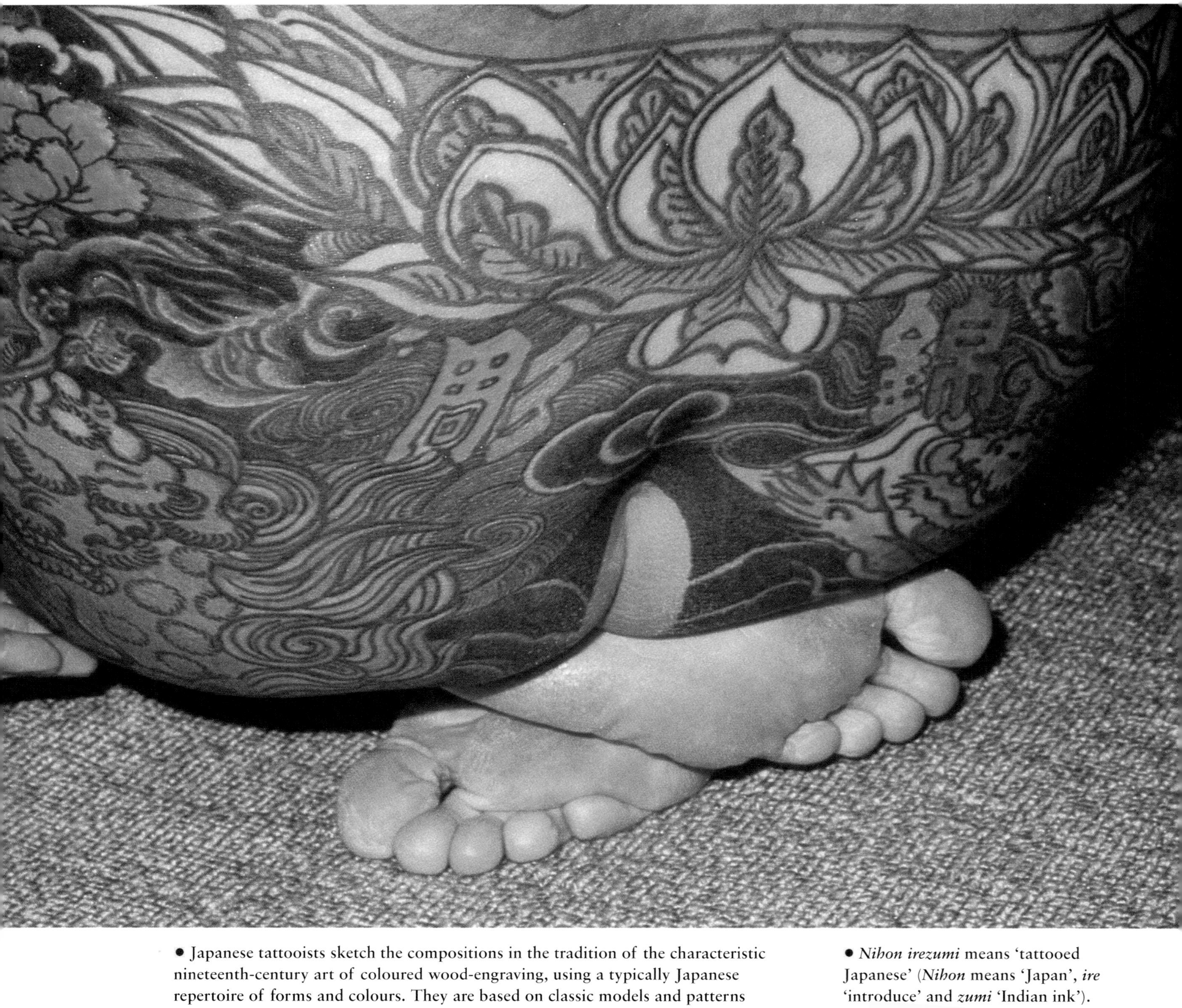

• Japanese tattooists sketch the compositions in the tradition of the characteristic nineteenth-century art of coloured wood-engraving, using a typically Japanese repertoire of forms and colours. They are based on classic models and patterns handed down – following the lines of the body, with particular attention to muscular movements. When the tattooed person moves his muscles the pictures come alive, and the Japanese bath brings out the brilliance of the colours.

• *Nihon irezumi* means 'tattooed Japanese' (*Nihon* means 'Japan', *ire* 'introduce' and *zumi* 'Indian ink').

-Wood Carvers were 1st tattoo artist. 17th Century
-Zenshin-bori
-1881 heir to English thorn had a dragon tat.

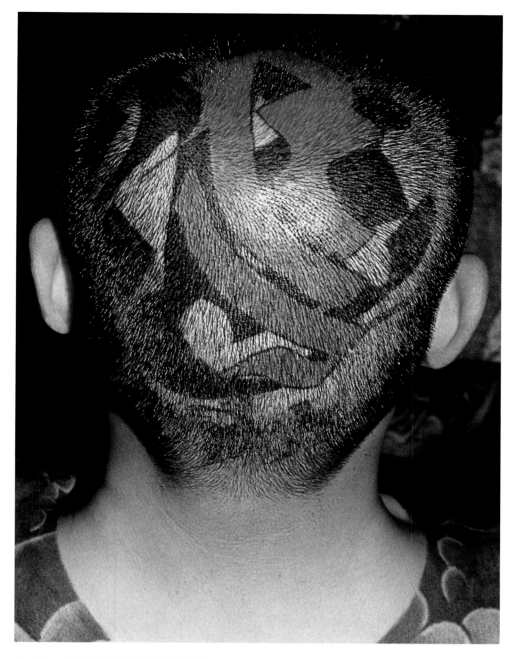

Only a few experts now do full tattooing in the old style: the transformation of the whole body into an intricate decorative sculpture. The patterns cover the back as far as the middle of the thighs and the whole of the front apart from a bare strip in the middle. With one session per week it can take over a year to complete the work. The traditional tools are bunches of needles set in wooden handles – between two and ten needles, according to the work to be done. The stylus, guided by the right hand is applied diagonally; the left hand, which also holds the paint brush between the middle and index fingers, stretches the skin. Previously only a few plant and mineral colours were used: a black which shines blue under the skin, red and brown. Modern chemical inks have opened up more varied colour possibilities.

Tradition in modernity: the photographs of Hideki Fujii

The history of erotic photography dates back to the nineteenth century in Japan. In the hand-coloured prints, produced mainly for tourists, attention was focused not on the depiction of the naked body so much as on the portrayal of the partly exposed female form – the interplay between the body and the colours and patterns of the artistically draped kimono was seen as alluring.

● The appeal of Fujii's pictures comes from the old Japanese tradition of white face-paint and the deliberate contrast between covered and exposed parts of the body.

For Hideki Fujii, colour magician and modern photographic artist, the attraction of the body is enhanced by its covering – in his case the 'clothing' consists of artistic painting, with traditional Japanese colours and shapes.

The faces, with their white make-up, are reminiscent of the artificial appearance of the geishas and their similarly 'empty' faces. Indeed, for the Japanese it is precisely their stylized, mask-like appearance that brings out the essence of beauty. This concept of artificial beauty is closely related to Zen Buddhism – which in Japan exerts a strong influence on poetry, painting and sculpture and also on everyday activities, and whose philosophy is expressed in, for example, the tea ceremony. Nature is seen as a spiritual phenomenon; its essence is only revealed through human intervention, through art. The shaping of patiently grown bonsai trees or the severe design of temple gardens are part of this tradition.

Body-painting, therefore, does not contradict nature, it improves on it. Fujii's art alludes to the centuries-old forms of Japanese body design, in which the human body is turned into a work of art by tattooing. He is also continuing the work of the Japanese masters of the coloured woodcut, whose stylized motifs were copied by the tattooists.

An important element in Fujii's pictures is the colour symbolism of Shinto, a religion in which nature plays a major part. The colour red, symbol of the rising sun and life, is particularly significant.

▶ The delicate play of coloured paints caresses the body like a silk kimono.

The Western world today: seeking the source

Decorated skin, as found in the modern industrialized society in the form of body-painting, tattooing and face make-up, can only rarely be traced back to its historical origins. Its archaic meaning has to a large extent been lost – though the made-up faces of actors, which still suggest a link with the ritual face-painting of antiquity, are an exception. Present day skin-decoration also shows that civilization has lost the capacity for unconscious creativity and change. Painted or tattooed bodies or made-up faces are now the expression of a purely artistic creative impulse – not an intuitive association with tradition, and certainly not a ritual ceremonial language. They are also not infrequently amateurish and unsophisticated displays born of an attempt to look different or to imitate.

One of the characteristics of civilization is that the potential of human creativity is led in different directions. On the one hand there is the independent artist, who, as it were, surrenders to his creativity in his work; on the other hand there is the 'amateur', who uses his creativity spontaneously and more or less randomly, playing with shapes and colours. The modern artist generally enters the creative process reflectively; the 'amateur' on the other hand usually trusts to his reflexes. Still discernible in the reflex is the naivety that the artist aspires to, as a Utopian ideal of harmony, is but he is no longer able to approach the sources of the art through prototypes and archetypes.

▲ The Berlin painter Elvira Bach at work. She only paints women and prefers a large, heavy type of woman with full breasts, whom she 'dresses' in high-heeled shoes. Bach sees the shoes not as an erotic symbol but as an expression of both strength and weakness.

◄ The painted body as a canvas for the imagination. But the change can only last for a few fleeting moments. Even as it is created its end is already in sight; the play of colours that took hours to compose is washed away in the shower. Body-painting thus becomes a synonym for the transience of man's creative impulse.

Body-painting as improvisation, polished artistic composition and perfect optical illusion

The skin as a surface for projecting fantasy: in body-painting, this is a concept that offers many different expressive possibilities, one of which is improvisation. Here the effect of body-painting comes from the excitement of the moment, the desire for permanent alteration. The converse is a body art which exhibits the person as the subject of a carefully planned artistic composition with a number of preparatory sketches. If these works are well-executed, they have great suggestive power. The variant of body-painting which creates a perfect optical illusion takes just as long to prepare and execute – for instance, a woman in a Harlequin costume painted on the skin in watercolours, or a man who appears to 'wear' a creased white shirt, tie and black trousers, but whose nakedness is hidden only by a briefcase, the only realistic feature in this mimicry. Appearance and reality, the old game, is enhanced by the surprise effect. But since body-painting as a transforming art is immediate and does not last, photography, film and video become documents of personal experience, reproductions of pictures. The body as a medium for creativity only survives through technology as a medium of conservation.

◄ *Yellow Untamed*, 1996. Using body-painting to rediscover our primitive nature and zest for life, distance ourselves from our everyday persona and allow an 'alien' side of ourselves to find expression: uncontrolled movements and voices can be surprising.

► The head and trunk of the female body are fused into a compositional unity of great visual elegance.

Colour brings out the inner person

Body-painting helps us regain contact with something inside us that is unfathomable, raw and untouched, something fundamentally and exclusively human that is waiting to be released and allowed to reveal itself. Not only do colours change a person's external appearance, they also change the inner man, who can now slough his 'old' skin and venture into and experience a new world. This creates a closer relationship between the external and internal levels of existence, in that we encounter a primeval reality within ourselves and at the same time get in touch with nature again: we both get in touch with our true selves and feel ourselves to be part of the whole. We should make room for what is wild, powerful, sensual and beautiful in our natures, re-establish contact with the power of the wind, the rustle of the trees, the strength of the rocks, the smell of the earth. The transformation is brought about by the process and the sensual experience of being painted, the 'comprehension' of nature all around, stones, trees, leaves, earth. At the same time, through being painted and through freedom of movement, we can also liberate ourselves from the straitjacket of self-judgment created by the advertising experts. Healing through body-painting: to be wild, different, to be yourself, to be at one with everyone and everything. We need these primitive living rituals in order once again to become part of nature, creation and the primordial.

▲ *Blue Bird*, 1996. A painting theme from a vision in a seance.

◄ *Snake Hanging from a Tree*, 1995. "Snake" was the basic theme of the person painted.

231

Body Art: hope of a reconciliation between art and life

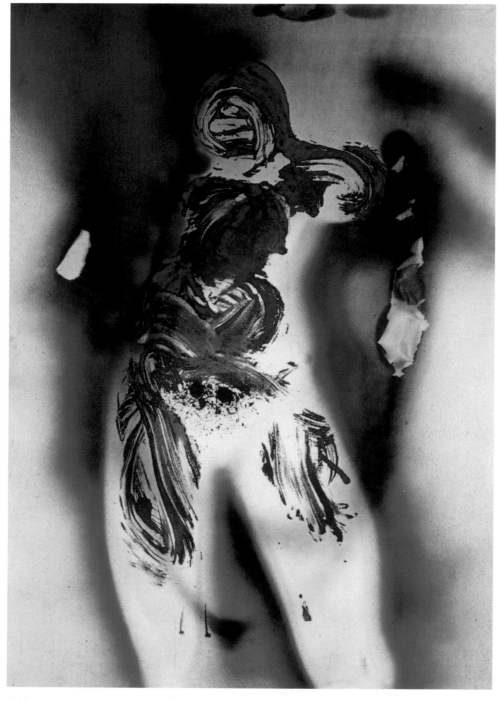

Although the terms body-painting and Body Art are generally used interchangeably, it seems appropriate to make a distinction between the two. Not that body-painting cannot be regarded as 'art'. But when Body Art is seen as a stylistic trend, it takes on an art-ideological dimension whose radicality sets it apart from body-painting. The ritualized painting found in Body Art is an attempt to reconcile art and life, as if to embody a myth, seeking to tap into a primordial, anarchic creative impulse and release human beings from the alienating influences of the consumer society. It has nothing to do with body-painting in the traditional sense, especially since the observer can no longer understand the intellectual demands of Body Art from the visual impression alone. This artificial world

● From the late 1950s Yves Klein (1928–1962) experimented with various materials and techniques, including body impressions on paper (anthropometries) and canvas (sudaria). The woman's body is a template (right), the silhouette of the imprint, which can be static or dynamic, is achieved by airbrushing (above). Klein, who called his models 'living paintbrushes' interpreted his art as a search for the intangible components of painting.

is usually difficult to comprehend without a detailed explanation. The Vienna actionist group around Hermann Nitsch, Otto Muehl and Günter Brus have established criteria for Body Art. In trying to achieve an archaic physicality they engage in cathartic rituals in which the breaking of taboos – in the form of painful mutilation, sadomasochistic practices, exhibitionism and other acts, right up to death by self-castration – is celebrated as the most radical form of self-expression. In this extreme form, in which provocativeness is taken to the limit of self-destruction, Body Art becomes a mirror of our alienation and longing for harmony, our loss of a primordial, archaic physicality.

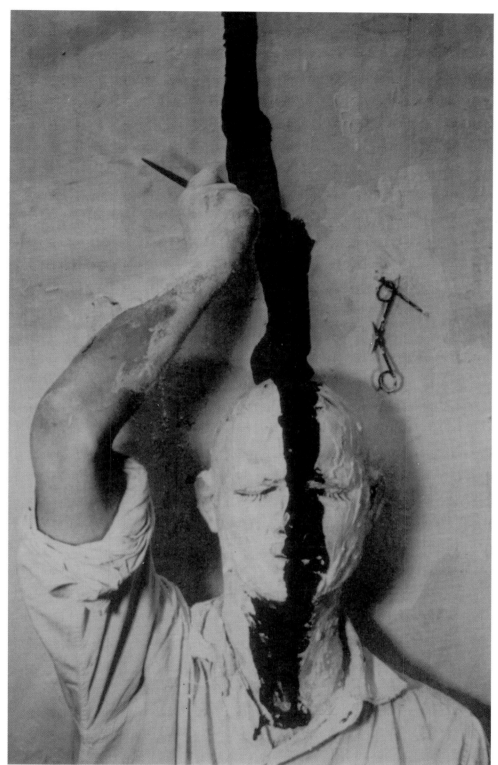

▲ Günter Brus (born 1938) is one of the founders of Viennese actionism. In his *Transfusion* (1965) he challenged the public with all the variants of his bodily excretions: a spectacular creation whose radicality was intended as a response to the pathology of the time. Brus's *Self-Painting* (1965) was based on similar ideas. The actionist of body art 'splits' his head, covered in white make-up, with a wide band of black paint. Brus's interpretation: 'Self-painting is controlled self-mutilation'.

Punks: colourful despair

● External appearance is particularly important in youth culture, and the young are always finding new ways of distinguishing themselves from the older generation.

To use appropriately colloquial terms, the way punks look is brilliant, fantastic, wicked. Clothes, body-ornaments and hairstyles are a visual signs of membership of a group that stress division and provocation. The punks favour leather gear with studs or ripped jeans, festoons of badges, chains and inflammatory symbols; the brightly coloured Mohawk haircut and other elaborate hairstyles are part of a head ornamentation so full of decorative possibilities that fantasy cannot set limits to it: make-up, chains, rings, clips and pins in ears, eyebrows and nose. Even tongues, lips and nipples – not to mention other parts of the body – are not immune. The decorated body becomes a demonstration of the counter-culture as shocking as its music: an expression of powerlessness in a competitive society that categorizes people according to certain criteria and lets anyone not conforming to them fall through the net.

The punks, who emerged at the end of the 1970s in Mrs Thatcher's Britain, set their own standards. This subculture's forms of expression through fashion and music might be seized upon by clever profiteers as a trend and successfully exploited commercially, but this does not hide the fact that it is more than just an aestheticization of provocative clichés. The crudeness and stridency have nothing essential to do with lifestyle; they are to be seen as a reaction, responding to exclusion from society with deliberate dissociation. The punk movement is not so much a way of life as a state of hopelessness – amplified with cynicism and derision, provocation and aggression in order to stifle despair. In piercing their skin and mutilating (and so stigmatizing) themselves, the punks are giving visible expression to the emotional pain that is associated with the meaning of the word punk: trash, rubbish.

● Punks as trend-setters of a teenage fashion that pronounced ripped or patched jeans to be the *dernier cri* of the sensibility of youth. The unconventional becomes a fashion accessory and the unusual a historical reference. The time devoted by punk girls to their make-up and coiffure is no less than that taken by aristocratic ladies in the Rococo period.

Tattooing: the hot needle under the skin

Obviously the effect of body-tattooing can now also be produced artificially by applying pigments. For tattoo artists, of course, this alternative is at least as absurd as the thought of a tattoo is for the average conventional citizen. What these people create with hot needles are works of art under the skin – zoological or botanical still-lifes, all kinds of fabulous creatures, historical paintings, autobiographical scenes or symbolic marks. The people who have their bodies illustrated in this way come from all walks of life – which does much to dispel the image of the tattooing trade as anti-bourgeois or even criminal. All over the world the tattooist's craft has an ancient and rich tradition from which, in the Far East for instance, a

● Tattooing may now have become socially acceptable, but it usually consists only of a small decorations involving a very few patterns; the main attraction of this form of body decoration lies in its intimacy. However, among fringe groups this intimacy of tattooing is swept away, and the whole body becomes a picture gallery.

recognized form of artistic expression has evolved.

There are as many reasons for deciding to have a tattoo as there are people. Self-affirmation, vanity or wishful thinking might be as important as the simple desire for decoration, the direct confirmation or rejection of moral concepts or an indication of social kinship and status. But the wish for an unalterable identity must always be father to the thought. It is not always achieved with a few patterns on the skin; some people have themselves 'woven' into a kind of living tapestry, others favour a made-to-measure 'skin garment' from head to foot – tattooing reflects the psychology of its wearer. And, for those whose urge for permanent markings is not satisfied by this form of body decoration, decoration can be burned into the skin with red-hot irons – branding.

● Tattooists now have their own trade fairs at which they display their art at international competitions, like that in Frankfurt in 1995.

Conflicting emotions: demonstrators and fans

▲ This Turkish football fan's colourful creation expresses his enthusiasm for his team at the 1996 European Cup.

Easter marches, peace marches, protests against rearmament and nuclear weapons, the fight against AIDS: at political demonstrations in recent years many participants, not content to express their protests with the usual banners, have used their own bodies. They are advertisements for their convictions; their faces, usually adorned with white or ash-coloured make-up, become symbols of menace, death and disaster. White makes the face rigid, conceals identity, covers the face like a shroud. But – just as white not only symbolizes fear but, at a carnival or on circus clowns, has a positive image, and in other contexts symbolizes innocence and purity – each colour has a range of possible meanings that are only apparent when related to a specific situation. Only

then does the colour acquire its peculiar and emotionally moving symbolic power. Football grounds, for instance, with their seething mass of people, are cauldrons of emotions where membership of a group and partisanship are indicated by clothing and flags – colourful scenarios of mass suggestion, polarized by hero-worship and abuse, which provide an outlet for the explosive forces of everyday life. Both players on the field and fans on the terraces make use of colours – the fans sometimes more than the players. And, however elaborate the fans' costumes, they only achieve their intended effect through incorporating club or national colours. It is thus that they convey the sense of group identity that is an essential part of the game.

▲ Free rein for the imagination: a fan at the 1994 World Cup who turned his head into a football.

◄ Costumes for passionate supporters. German fans wearing the national colours dancing to celebrate victory in a regional match.

Carnival: a short scherzo

▲ The tradition of the courtly masquerade can still be seen in the masked processions at the Swabian-Alemannic Shrovetide festival.

The origins of carnival are buried deep in history. They lie in the winter and spring festivals of ancient Rome and Byzantium and in the customs of the late Middle Ages. Whether it was carnival (*carne vale*: 'farewell to meat') or the Shrovetide festival before Lent, with its variety of regional traditions, there was always an officially sanctioned special period before the fasting began in which – as in the Roman Saturnalia – the barriers of status and class were removed and a kind of 'Christian Bacchanalia' was permitted, with lavish feasting and dancing, plays and masked processions. It was a festival which, as Goethe once wrote, 'is not really given to the people but which the people give themselves'. Crude mockery and blasphemous or obscene performances were common: carnival as a controlled public explosion.

In the same vein was the fifteenth-century Shrovetide play, which used not only to delight its audience with exaggerated parodies and sexually explicit language, but later also made satirical attacks on politics and religion. Shrovetide, carnival – a time of revelry punctuating the year, a brief scherzo in which the street becomes a stage. Rudiments of the historic Shrovetide festival can still be found today in Germany – for instance in the dance of the Munich market women (medieval), the Swabian-Alemannic mask parades (late Baroque), the fancy dress, carnival orations and Shrove Monday processions (from the time of the Metternich restoration). Although the present-day carnivals have become so commercial and highly organized that they have lost much of their immediacy and spontaneity, wherever the popular festival does not organize the public but encourages them to take an active

part it has certainly retained all its vitality. Then the carnival becomes a colourful masquerade that disguises bodies and unveils fantasies. Through playing a role people can experience a transformation which takes them out of themselves.

▶ Abstract painting on a joyful face. The eyes sparkle: *carpe diem!*

▼ When you try to paint your face, all that restricts you is your imagination.

Make-up: part camouflage, part identification

Since ancient times people all over the world have used make-up to alter their external appearance and express their sense of beauty. The versatility of a made-up face as a medium for self-expression never ceases to amaze – not only because of the way it enhances the various expressions of human mimicry but also, above all, because powder, paint, creams and beauty treatments allow people to 'make something of themselves' (today more than ever before).

Modern women make themselves up as a matter of course every day, just as they put on clothes. To be sure, men (with a few exceptions) have not felt the need to wear make-up since the Rococo period, but even they now have to do so when getting ready for a television appearance. Faces are less likely to be seen 'naked and unadorned' on that medium than anywhere else in everyday life.

Before you can seduce with the aid of make-up you must be seduced into wearing make-up – so 'in the beginning was advertising'. Because it suggests an ideal of beauty, reinforced by the use of models and film stars, it determines fashion trends, which explains why people use make-up. But the customers also hope to firm up their self-confidence along with their skin. Ultimately it is not just a matter of persuading waverers to use creams but of selling cosmetics as a miracle weapon against ageing. The dream is to be flawless. Some make-up might melt mercilessly in the rush to conform, but, at a time when the aesthetic demands of the cult of youth and its emphasis on the body can even determine one's career

◄ How hair, make-up and accessories can alter a face: five variations on the same woman.

prospects, the façade of make-up can increasingly blur the distinction between disguise and identity. The beautician, a new professional, tries even then to build up what the body is already breaking down. Appearance determines awareness!

▲ *Marina Paints Luciano*, by Franz Gertsch, 1975. Role reversal: this picture in the photo-realist style shows a masculine-looking woman making up the feminine-looking artist Luciano Castelli. For Castelli the performance aspect of making up is particularly important. Applying and removing the artistic painting is part of the ritual.

243

The microcosm of clowns

The hero of Thomas Mann's novel *Felix Krull* marvelled at clowns: 'ageless, adolescent sons of foolishness'; 'alien jokers . . . with their chalk-white faces made up to look as buffoonish as possible . . . masks, in other words, which are in singular contrast to the splendour of their costumes'. Felix Krull must have been especially fascinated by the so-called white-face clown, the descendant of Harlequin, because he only mentions the auguste in passing, even though the latter, with his torrent of words and his grotesque baggy costume, invites all the attention.

Both of them – the intelligent and arrogant white-face clown and the optimistic and noisy auguste – go together, like Laurel and Hardy in slapstick, to make a pair of heavenly twins of circus comedy, achieving their effects through contrast. Many specific forms and specializations have developed in the art of clowning, but

◄ The famous Charlie Rivel, who for decades delighted his audience through changing his normal face for his clown's make-up. He has not yet put on the bald wig with the fringe of bright red hair and the cube-shaped metal nose.

the traditional model has lost none of its appeal. The white-face and the auguste are archetypes: intellectual pride set against naive artfulness, authority and order in conflict with anarchy and lightheartedness. The resulting comedy also casts shadows, and the reconciliation of the contrasts remains a myth.

The solo acts by the great clowns are not mythical but emotionally moving; they create a microcosm of the world in the arena, using body language, mimicry, make-up and props, producing that difficult-to-define comedy which only acquires its characteristic flavour from its interplay of various moods. This is the supreme art of the clown. Playing upon the whole range of human emotions, he combines light-hearted comedy with dreaminess, tenderness and even an unsentimental melancholy. Comedy has as many masks as laughter has expressions.

▼ White-face and auguste clowns in the ring. The contrast between the two types derives not only from their actions and body language but also, in particular, from their different make-up.

▲ The elegant sweeping black line above one eyebrow gives the pale face of the white-face clown something of that intellectual arrogance that is also found in Gustaf Gründgens' famous Mephisto make-up.

The imaginative power of make-up in the theatre

▲ Scene from Shakespeare's *Richard II* in a performance by the Théâtre du Soleil. The make-up and costumes are based on the Japanese kabuki theatre, which reinforces the alienating effect.

◄ Goethe's *Faust*: Gustaf Gründgens in his famous Mephisto make-up.

The theatre is not a representation but a simile of human forms of expression. For two-and-a-half millennia the actor has been at the centre of a world which binds him to a plot and a setting and lifts him out of everyday reality with face-paint and costumes, scenery and lighting. Although in Greek antiquity the theatre (the word means 'a show place') evolved from its Dionysian religious origins into a world art form, it has continued over the centuries to have what is in essence a religious effect – because the stage has always depended on ritualization. This is sometimes reinforced nowadays by non-European influences, although, on the other hand, since realism, it has also tried to master new styles. The painted masks of make-up show the ritual nature of theatre. They replaced the sculpted masks in the middle ages, and yet, like them, they represent the imaginative power that only takes over when barriers are crossed.

Bibliography

General

Brain, R., *The Decorated Body* (London, Hutchinson, 1979)

Chefs d'oeuvre du Musée de l'Homme (Paris, Caisse Nationale des Monuments Historiques et des Sites, 1965)

Ebin, V., *The Body Decorated* (London, Thames and Hudson, 1979)

Feest, C., *The Art of War* (London, Thames and Hudson, 1980)

Lenars, C., J. Lenars and A. Vivel, *Corps en tête* (Paris, Draeger, 1979)

Leuzinger, E., *Die Kunst der Naturvölker* (Berlin, Propyläen, 1978)

Malraux, A., *The Psychology of Art* (London, A. Zwemmer, 1949)

Roy, C., *Arts Sauvages* (Paris, Robert Delpire, 1957)

Rubin, A., *Marks of Civilization, Artistic Transformations of the Human Body* (Los Angeles, Museum of Cultural History, University of California Press, 1988)

Sydow, E. von, *Die Kunst der Naturvölker und der Vorzeit* (Berlin, Propyläen, 1938)

Thévoz, M., *Der bemalte Körper* (Zurich, ABC, 1985)

Theye, T., *Der geraubte Schatten, Die Photographie als ethnographisches Dokument* (Munich, C.J. Bucher, 1989)

The Magic of Colours

Breasted, J.H., *A History of Egypt from the Earliest Times to the Persian Conquest* (London and New York, Hodder & Stoughton, 1950)

Chamoux F., *The Civilization of Greece* (London, George Allen & Unwin, 1965)

Idole, frühe Götterbilder und Opfergaben (Mainz, Prähistorische Staatssammlung München, 1985)

Licht, H., *Sittengeschichte Griechenlands* (Reinbek bei Hamburg, Rowohlt, 1969)

Marinatos, S., *Kreta, Thera und das mykenische Hellas* (Munich, Hirmer, 1986)

Posener, G., *Dictionnaire de la Civilisation Égyptienne* (Paris, Hazan, 1939)

Striedter, K.H., *Felsbilder in der Sahara* (Munich, Prestel-Verlag, 1984)

America

Anton, F., *Ancient Mexican Art* (London, Thames and Hudson, 1970)

——*Art of the Maya* (London, Thames and Hudson, 1970)

——*The Art of Ancient Peru* (London, Thames and Hudson, 1972)

——*Ancient Peruvian Textiles* (London, Thames and Hudson, 1987)

Baer, G., *Reise und Forschung in Ost-Peru*, reprinted from *Verhandlungen der Naturforschenden Gesellschaft in Basel*, vol. 80/2 (Basel, 1969)

Bancroft-Hunt, N., and W. Forman, *People of the Totem, The Indians of the Pacific Northwest* (London, Orbis, 1979)

Bisilliat, M., *Xingu, Tribal Territory*, text by Orlando and Claudio Villas-Bôas (London, Collins, 1979)

Catlin, G., *Letters and Notes on the Manners, Customs and Conditions of the North American Indians*, 2 vols (New York, Dover Publications, 1973)

Dockstader, F.J., *The Kachina and the White Man* (Albuquerque, University of New Mexico Press, 1985)

Douglas, F.H., and R. d'Harnoncourt, *Indian Art of the United States* (New York, Museum of Modern Art, 1941)

Haberland, W., *Die Kunst des indianischen Amerika* (Zurich, Museum Rietberg, 1971)

——*Amerikanische Archäologie* (Darmstadt, Wissenschaftliche Buchgesellschaft, 1991)

Hartmann, G., *Litjoko, Puppen der Karaja, Brasilien* (Berlin, Museum für Völkerkunde, Staatliche Museen Preussischer Kulturbesitz, 1973)

Hartmann, H., *Die Plains- und Prärieindianer Nordamerikas* (Berlin, Museum für Völkerkunde, Staatliche Museen Preussischer Kulturbesitz, 1974)

Hassrick, R.B., *The Colourful Story of North American Indians* (London, Octopus, 1975)

Holm, B., *A Century of Northwest Coast Indian Art at the Burke Museum*, Thomas Burke Memorial, Washington State monograph no. 4 (Seattle, 1987)

Humboldt, A. von, *Relation Historique du Voyage aux Régions Équinoxiales du Nouveau Continent* (Paris, 1814–27)

Hurst, D., *et al.*, *Die Welt der Indianer* (Munich, Frederking & Thaler, 1994)

Indianer der Prärien und Plains. Reisen und Sammlungen des Herzogs Paul Wilhelm von Württemberg (1822–24) und des Prinzen Maximilian zu Wied (1832–34) (Stuttgart, Linden-Museum, Staatliches Museum für Völkerkunde, 1987)

Indianer des Amazonas (Munich, Staatliches Museum für Völkerkunde, 1960)

Josephy, A. M., *The American Heritage Book of Indians* (New York, American Heritage, 1961)

——*500 Nations. An Illustrated History of North American Indians* (London, Hutchinson/Pimlico, 1995)

King, J.C.H., *Portrait Masks from the Northwest Coast of America* (London, Thames and Hudson, 1979)

Martius, C.F.P. von, *Brasilianische Reise 1817–1820* (Frankfurt am Main, 1994, and Munich, 1995, Schirn Kunsthalle and Staatliches Museum für Völkerkunde)

Ricciardi, M., *Vanishing Amazon* (London, Weidenfeld & Nicolson, 1991)

Stirling, M.W., *National Geographic on Indians of the Americas* (Washington DC, National Geographic Society, 1955)

Trupp, F., *Amazonas* (Vienna and Munich, Schroll, 1983)

Verswijver, G., *Kaiapó* (Tervuren, Musée royal d'Afrique Centrale, 1992)

Villas-Bôas, O., and C. Villas-Bôas, *Xingú*, 2 vols (Porto Alegre, Kuarup, 1984 and 1988)

Waldman, C., *Atlas of the North American Indians* (New York and London, Facts on File, 1985)

Wied, M., Prinz zu, *Reise in das Innere Nord-America in den Jahren 1832 bis 1834* (Koblenz, J. Hoelscher, 1839)

Xingú, Unter Indianern in Zentral-Brasilien, Zur einhundertjährigen Wiederkehr der Erforschung des Rio Xingú durch Karl von den Steinen (Berlin, Museum für Völkerkunde, Staatliche Museen Preussischer Kulturbesitz, 1986)

Zerries, O., *Unter Indianern Brasiliens, Sammlung Spix und Martius 1817–1820*, vol. 1 of *Sammlungen aus dem Staatlichen Museum für Völkerkunde München* (Innsbruck and Frankfurt am Main, Pinguin and Umschau-Verlag, 1980)

Oceania

Barrow, T., *An Illustrated Guide to Maori Art* (Auckland, Methven Publications New Zealand, 1984)

Brake, B., J. McNeish and D. Simmons, *Art of the Pacific* (New York, Abrams, 1979)

Cook, J., and J. King, *Logs and Journals, Third Voyage. A Voyage to the Pacific Ocean*, 4 vols (London, John Stockdale, 1784)

Guiart, J., *Ozeanien* (Munich, Beck, 1963)

Joest, W., *Tätowiren* (Berlin, 1887)

Kelm, H., *Kunst vom Sepik*, 3 vols (Berlin, Museum für Völkerkunde, Staatliche Museen Preussischer Kulturbesitz, 1966–68)

Lommel, A., *Motiv und Variation in der Kunst des zircumpazifischen Raumes*

(Munich, Staatliches Museum für Völkerkunde, 1962)

Meyer, A.J.P., *Ozeanische Kunst*, 2 vols (Cologne, Könemann, 1995)

Robley, Major-General, *'Moko', or Maori Tattooing* (London, Chapman & Hall, 1896)

Schmitz, C.A., *Ozeanische Kunst, Skulpturen aus Melanesien* (Munich, Akanthus, 1962)

Stazecka, D.C., and A.L. Cranstone, *The Solomon Islands* (London, British Museum, 1974)

Steinen, K. von den, *Die Marquesaner und ihre Kunst*, 3 vols (Berlin, Dietrich Reimer, 1925–28)

Stingl, M., *Kunst der Südsee* (Leipzig, Seemann-Verlag, 1985)

Strathern, M., and A. Strathern, *Self-Decoration in Mount Hagen* (London, Duckworth, 1970)

Tischner, H., *Kunst der Südsee* (Hamburg, Hauswedall, 1954)

Australia

Berndt, R.M., and E.S. Phillips, *The Australian Aboriginal Heritage, An Introduction through the Arts*, 2 vols (Sydney, Australian Society for Education through the Arts, 1973)

Brandl, E., *Australian Aboriginal Paintings in Western and Central Arnhem Land* (Canberra, Australian Institute of Aboriginal Studies, 1973)

Die Kultur der Traumzeit, Tradition und Gegenwart der Aborigines Australiens (Freiburg im Breisgau, Museum für Völkerkunde, 1991)

Lommel, A., and K. Lommel, *Die Kunst des fünften Erdteils* (Munich, Staatliches Museum für Völkerkunde, 1959)

——*Die Kunst des alten Australiens* (Munich, Prestel-Verlag, 1989)

McCarthy, F.D., *Australian Aboriginal Rock Art* (Sydney, Australian Museum, 1958)

Neale, M., and M. Neale, *Yiribana, Aboriginal and Torres Strait Islander Collection* (Sydney, Art Gallery of New South Wales, 1994)

Ryan, J., *Paint up Big, Warlpiri Women's Art of Lajamanu* (Melbourne, National Gallery of Victoria, 1988)

Africa

Adler, F., *Kenia* (Munich, List, 1984)

Bamert, A., *Afrika, Stammeskunst in Urwald und Savanne* (Olten and Freiburg im Breisgau, Walter, 1980)

Baumann, H., *Die Völker Afrikas und ihre traditionellen Kulturen*, 2 vols (Wiesbaden, Steiner-Verlag, 1975)

Beckwith, C., *Maasai* (New York, Abrams, 1980)

——*Nomads of Niger* (New York, Abrams, 1983)

Beckwith, C., and A. Fisher, *African Ark, Peoples of the Horn* (London, Collins and Harvill, 1990)

Castiglioni, A., and A. Castiglione, *Adams schwarze Kinder* (Zurich, Schweizer Verlagshaus, 1981)

Errington, S., *Völker der Wildnis, Krieger des Weissen Nils* (Amsterdam, Time-Life, 1982)

Fantin, M., *Senufo e Baule, Arti Grafiche* (Trento, R. Mantrini, 1965)

Faik-Nzuji, C., *Die Macht des Sakralen, Mensch, Natur und Kunst in Afrika* (Solothurn and Düsseldorf, Walter, 1993)

Faris, J.C., *Nuba Personal Art* (London, Duckworth, 1972)

——*Southeast Nuba Social Relations* (Aachen, Alano, 1989)

Fisher, A., *Afrika im Schmuck* (Cologne, DuMont Buchverlag, 1984)

Krieg, K.-H., *Podai, Bemalte Körper – Bemalte Häuser* (Hamburg Museum für Völkerkunde, 1995)

Magor, T., *African Warriors* (London, Harvill Press, 1994)

Maurin Garcia, M., *Le Henné, Plante du paradis* (Geneva, Georges Naef, 1992)

Meauzé, P., *African Art, Sculpture* (London, Weidenfeld & Nicolson, 1968)

Ricciardi, M., *Vanishing Africa* (London, Collins & Harvill, 1971)

Riefenstahl, L., *The People of Kau* (London, Collins, 1976)

Schmalenbach, W., *Die Kunst Afrikas* (Basel, Holbein, 1953)

——*Afrikanische Kunst aus der Sammlung Barbier-Mueller, Genf* (Munich, Prestel-Verlag, 1988)

India, Nepal and Indonesia

Fischer, E., and H. Shah., *Kunsttraditionen in Nordindien, Stammeskunst, Volkskunst, klassische Kunst* (Zurich, Museum Rietberg, 1972)

——'Tatauieren in Kutch', in *Ethnologische Zeitschrift* (Zurich) II, 1973, pp. 105–129.

Ganolhi, I., *Eternal India* (London, Allen & Unwin, 1978)

Hartsuiker, D., *Sádhus, Holy Men of India* (London, Thames and Hudson, 1993)

Icke-Schwalbe, L., and M. Günther, *Andamanen und Nikobaren, Ein Kulturbild der Inseln im Indischen Meer* (Dresden and Münster, Lit-Verlag, 1991)

Koch, P., and H. Stegmüller, *Geheimnisvolles Nepal, Buddhistische und hinduistische Feste* (Munich, List, 1983)

Kramrisch, S., *Indische Kunst* (London, Phaidon, 1968)

Samson, L., and A. Parsrieha, *Der klassische indische Tanz* (Sachsenheim, Burg, 1987)

Schefold, Reimar, *Spielzeug für die Seelen* (Zurich, Museum Rietberg, 1980)

China and Japan

Alley, R., *Peking Opera* (Beijing, New World Press, 1984)

Böller, W., *Meisterwerke des japanischen Farbholzschnitts* (Olten, Graf, 1957)

Cheng, J., *Gesichter der Peking-Oper* (Hamburg, Christians, 1990)

Cobb, J., *Geisha, The Life, the Voices, the Art* (New York, Knopf, 1995)

Feddersen, M., *Japanisches Kunsthandwerk* (Munich, Klinkhardt & Biermann, 1983)

Hideki Fujii, *Karada Kesho* (Tokyo, Niho Geijutsu, 1984)

Kindermann, H., *Einführung in das asiatische Theater* (Vienna, Böhlau, 1985)

Leroi-Gourhan, A., and A. Leroi-Gourhan, *Un Voyage chez les Aïnous, Hokkaïdo - 1938* (Paris, Albin Michel, 1989)

Naberfeld, P.E., *Kurzgefasste Geschichte Japans* (Tokyo and Hamburg, Deutsche Gesellschaft für Natur- und Völkerkunde, 1965)

Rathgen, K., *Staat und Kultur der Japaner*, Monographien zur Weltgeschichte (Leipzig, Velhagen & Klasing, 1907)

Richie, D., and I. Buruma, *The Japanese Tattoo* (New York and Tokyo, Weatherhill, 1980)

Shinoyama Kishin, *Tamasaburo Bandô* (Tokyo and New York, Kodansha, 1978)

Smith, Bradley, *Japan, a History in Art* (London, Weidenfeld & Nicolson, 1964)

Vanis, K., *Schüler des Birngartens, Das chinesische Singspiel* (Prague, Artia, 1956)

The Western World Today

Bruno, C., *Tatoués, qui êtes-vous...?* (Paris, Brodard et Taupin, 1970)

Fellowes, C.H., *The Tattoo Book* (Princeton NJ, Pyne Press, 1971)

Lazi, C., *The Tattoo, Graffiti for the Soul* (London, Sunburst, 1994)

Sommer, V., *Feste, Mythen, Rituale* (Hamburg, Geo/Gruner & Jahr, 1992)

Webb, S., *Heavily Tattooed – Men and Women* (New York, McGraw Hill, 1976)

Wroblewski, C., *Tattoo, Pigments of Imagination* (London, W.H. Allen, 1987)

——*Skin Shows, the Art of Tattoo* (London, Virgin, 1989, 1991 and 1993)

Sources of illustrations

Photographs

Adler, Florian: 153
Ferdinand Anton archive, Munich: 26,
  28, 29, 30, 31 bottom, 32, 33 top left
  and bottom left, 35, 36, 37 left, 39 top
  left and bottom left, 40, 41, 48, 49
  bottom right, 56 right, 65 bottom left,
  92, 93
Asselberghs, Roger/Barbier-Mueller
  Museum, Geneva: 165 right
Asselberghs, Roger/© AFRICA-
  MUSEUM Tervuren (Belgium): 114
Athens, National Archaeological
  Museum: 25 bottom left.
Auckland, City Art Gallery (Partridge
  collection): 96
© Bachman, Bill: 107 top
Barbey, Bruno/MAGNUM/FOCUS: 122
  bottom
Basel, Museum der Kulturen: 81 bottom
  right, 86 right
Bavaria Bildagentur/Picture Finders: 107
  bottom left
© Becker-Rau, Christel: 198
Beckwith, Carol/Robert Estall
  Photographs: 124, 155, 156, 157
Beckwith, Carol and Angela
  Fisher/Robert Estall Photographs: 126,
  127, 128, 129, 130, 131, 134, 149
Berlin: Staatliche Museen zu Berlin –
  Preussischer Kulturbesitz/Museum für
  Völkerkunde: 89 right, 119 right
© Bisilliat, Maureen: 57, 58, 59 left, 60
  right, 61 left
Blum, Dieter/© STERN: 227
Bossemeyer, Klaus/BILDERBERG: 245
  right
Brake, Brian/RAPHO/FOCUS: 85, 88,
  98, 99
Bremen, Überseemuseum: 84 bottom left
Brus, Günter: 233 right
Budapest, Néprajzi Muzeum – Museum
  of Ethnography: 80 left, 84 top right
Cobb, Jodi (from *Geisha* by Jodi Cobb,
  © 1995 Jodi Cobb, by kind permission
  of Alfred A. Knopf Inc., New York):
  210, 212, 213
Cologne, Museum Ludwig, Rheinisches
  Bildarchiv: 243
Couturiaux, Albert, National
  Geographic Image Collection: 137 top
  left
Degen, Thomas: 175 right, 234
DPA – Deutsche Presse Agentur GmbH:
  244/45 bottom
© Ediciones Poligrafa S. A.: 163

Eisenstaedt, Alfred/LIFE MAGAZINE,
  © Time Inc.: 176
Errington, Sarah (from *Völker der
  Wildnis: Krieger des Weissen Nils*,
  Amsterdam, Time-Life, 1982): 148
© Mme Fain: 219 right
Feurer, Hans: 226
Fievet-Demont, Jeanette: 133
Fischer, Eberhard, Rietberg Museum,
  Zurich: 188, 189
Fisher, Angela/Robert Estall
  Photographs: 120, 125
Franck, Martine/MAGNUM/FOCUS:
  246/247
Glinn, Burt/MAGNUM/FOCUS: 174,
  207, 214, 215 right
Grassmann, Rosel (Photography and
  Body-painting): 228, 230, 231
Gröning, Dörte: 100, 105, 240, 244 top
  left, 244 bottom left
Hamburg, Museum für Völkerkunde: 84
  bottom right
Claus & Liselotte Hansmann, Historico-
  cultural picture archive, Munich: 20,
  21, 22 left, 23, 24, 37 right, 38, 39
  bottom right, 42, 44 left, 45, 50, 51
  right, 64 left, 66 left, 67, 86 left, 95
  bottom right, 119 left, 162, 164,
  178/179, 215 left, 220 left
Harrer, Heinrich: 193 bottom
Held, André: 132 centre and right
Heusch, Luc de: 115 right
Hideki Fujii: 224, 225
Hinz, Hans: 25 top right
Hinz, Volker/© STERN: 173
Hodges, Christopher: 107 bottom right
Hourticolon, Dirk: 177
Kirk, Malcolm S.: 4/5, 70, 72, 73, 74, 75,
  77 right and top left, 82, 83, 94 left, 95
  bottom left, 184, 184/185, 205, 209, 211
Koch, Peter: 182, 183 right top and
  bottom
Krieg, Karl-Heinz: 168, 169
Lazi, Claudio: 236, 237, 236/237 top
Leidmann, Bert: 150 right
Lenars, Josette & Charles/EXPLORER,
  Vanves: 103 bottom left and right, 111,
  117 right, 178 left
London, © British Museum: 106 left, 118
  left, 132 left
Luz, Horst: 135
Magor, Thomasin (photograph from
  African Warriors, London, Harvill,
  1994; © Thomasin Magor 1994.
  Reproduced by kind permission of
  The Harvill Press): 152
Mangold, Guido: 200

Marika, Mawalan: 104 right
Mason, Linda (Photographer & Make-
  up Artist) with Linda Mason Elements
  Cosmetics, Actress Suzanna Midnight,
  Hairstylist Cynthia for John Sahag:
  242
Maurin Garcia, Michèle/Edito Georges
  Naef S.A.: 121, 123
Meyer, Claus C./DAS FOTOARCHIV,
  Essen: 52, 54, 55, 60 left, 61 right, 62
  bottom, 63 top
Munich, Staatliches Museum für
  Völkerkunde: 187 left
Nachtwey, James/MAGNUM/FOCUS:
  161
Ortega, Maurice, Australian Museum,
  Sydney: 89 left
Paris, Réunion des Musées Nationaux:
  87 right, 90 top left, 90 right, 91
Peter, Hanns: 78, 79, 103 top
Peter Horner: 180, 181
Peyer, Fritz: 241, 246 left
Pinson, C./EXPLORER, Vanves: 103
  bottom centre
Rauchensteiner, Hans: 238, 239, 238/239
Reininger, Alon/CONTACT/FOCUS: 65
  top
Reiser, Andreij/BILDERBERG: 221
Ricciardi, Mirella: 13, 14, 15, 154, 170
Richter, Stefan, Copyright © Stefan
  Richter/All rights reserved: 179 right
Riefenstahl, Leni: 6/7, 9, 112/113, 138,
  139, 140, 141, 142, 143, 144, 145, 146,
  147, 151, 166, 222, 223
Schäfer, Petra Maria/© STERN: 229
Schalkwijk, Bob (from *DU*, no. 6, 1966):
  12
Schefold, Reimar: 194/195, 195, 196, 197
Schulthess, Emil/Emil Schulthess Erben,
  Photoarchiv, Zurich: 160
© Stede, Clark: 190, 191, 192 top, 193
  top
Stingl, Miloslav: 84 bottom right, 106
  right
Striedter, Karl Heinz: 18, 19
Toronto, Royal Ontario Museum –
  Musée Royal de l'Ontario: 34
Tweedie, Penny: 104 left
Ullal, Jay/© STERN: 186
Vaniš, Josef: 202 right, 203, 204 left, 206
  right, 208/209
© Verswijver, Gustaaf: 59 right
© VG Bild-Kunst, Bonn 1996, Yves Klein:
  232, 233 bottom left
© Wolfe, Art: 1, 2/3, 102
Winterthur, Delaware, Henry Francis du
  Pont Winterthur Museum: 43

Wipperfürth, Olaf/Könemann
Verlagsgesellschaft mbH, © 1995: 77
bottom left
Todd Friedman,
www.TFPhoto.com,tfp@
TFPhoto.com, **Daniel Woijik**: 235 top
left

Drawings

Pferdmenges-Gröning, Gisela: 31 top, 44
right, 45 left, 49 top left, centre and
right, 49 bottom left, 62 top left,
centre and right, 63 bottom, 76, 81 top
and bottom left, 117 top and bottom
left, 122 top, 146/147, 158 bottom
right, 188 top, 192 bottom, 201, 202
left, 204 right, 206 left, 208 left,
(copies after photos by Shinoyama
Kishin from *Tamasaburo Bandô*,
Tokyo and New York, 1978) 216 and
217
17: Reconstruction by Henri Lhote of a
rock painting
33 right top and bottom: After
photographs by Hans Ruedi Dörig
66 right top and bottom: From O.
Zerries, *Unter Indianern Brasiliens:
Sammlung Spix und Martius
1817–1820* (Innsbruck and Frankfurt
am Main, 1980)
94 right and 95 top: After drawings from
Karl von den Steinen, *Die
Marquesaner und ihre Kunst* (Berlin,
1925–28)
97 top left: From Major-General Robley:
'*Moko*' *or Maori Tattooing* (London,
1896)
97 top centre: C. M. Praetorius, British
Museum, *Studio Magazine*, 1900,
from T. Barrow, *An Illustrated Guide
to Maori Art* (Auckland, 1984)
97 bottom right: From J. Cook and J.
King, *A Voyage to the Pacific Ocean*
(London, 1784)
97 top right: From W. Joest, *Tätowiren*
(Berlin 1887)
108, 109 right, 109 left: After E. Brandl,
*Australian Aboriginal Paintings in
Western and Central Arnhem Land*
(Canberra, 1973)
134 right: After T. J. M. Chappel in A.
Rubin, *Marks of Civilization: Artistic
Transformations of the Human Body*
(Los Angeles, 1988)
165 left: After R. C. Abraham in A.
Rubin, *Marks of Civilization: Artistic
Transformations of the Human Body*
(Los Angeles, 1988)
168: From K.-H. Krieg, *Podai: Bemalte
Körper – Bemalte Häuser* (Hamburg,
Museum für Völkerkunde, 1995)
202/203: After an original by Josef
Vaniš.
219 centre: After Obora Kazuo in A.
Rubin, *Marks of Civilization: Artistic
Transformations of the Human Body*
(Los Angeles, 1988)

Gröning Archive

PHOTOGRAPHS

81 top right, 115 bottom left, 116, 118
right, 136, 137 right, 137 bottom left,
175 bottom left, 183 top left, 220
right, 56 left (George Holton), 90
bottom left (Karl Muller), 115 top left
and 150 left (Arnold Bamert), 167
(Franco Cianetti), 175 top left (Peter
Brahm), 187 right (Raghubir Singh),
218 (Franco Cianetti), 219 bottom left
(Fosco Maraini), 235 (Tom Picton)

DRAWINGS

22 right, 25 top left, 46, 47, 51 (Museum
of the American Indian, New York),
80 right, 87 left, 158 left (after a
photograph from *Epocha* in the
1960s), 159 left (after a photograph
from *National Geographic Magazine*,
1937), 159 right (after a photograph
by Herbert Lang, 1910, The American
Museum of Natural History, New
York)

Maps

Theiss Heidolph, Eching

The editor, Karl Gröning, and the
originating publishers, Frederking &
Thaler, have made every effort to
identify all holders of rights in the
illustrations in order to obtain the
necessary permissions and to include the
appropriate acknowledgment in the list
of sources. Unfortunately this has not
been possible in a few cases. Holders of
any such rights are invited to bring the
matter to the attention of Frederking &
Thaler Verlag GmbH, Georgenstrasse 70,
80799 Munich, Germany.

Acknowledgments

First of all, thanks are due to Eva Neurath, chairman of Thames and Hudson. Twenty years ago, when I was still very new to the publishing world, I called on her with the publisher Heinrich Maria Ledig-Rowohlt to show her two project proposals. Her kindness and her understanding smiles at the loose sheets with which I was trying to present my ideas for books are something I have never forgotten, and they were to be the incentive for a great many books. My gratitude is all the greater because the English translation of this book is being published by her company.

My thanks go also to the many people who have helped me with advice, practical support and relevant material. I should like to mention some of them by name:

Dr Eberhart Fischer, Director of the Rietberg Museum, Zurich

Dr Frederick J. Dockstader, former Director of the Museum of the American Indian, New York

Gerhard Henze, New York

Dr Thomas Hölscher, art historian, Munich

Dr Maria Kecskesi, Head of the African Department at the State Museum of Ethnology, Munich

Karl-Heinz Krieg, African art expert, the fruits of whose five research trips to Guinea have provided a great deal of information on modern body-painting in Africa

The late Prof. Elsy Leuzinger, lecturer in non-European art, Zurich

Dr Wulf Lohse, Head of the African Department at the Museum of Ethnology, Hamburg

The late Robert Schäfer, publisher, List Verlag and Südwest Verlag

Prof. Reimar Schefold, Rijksuniversiteit, Leiden

Dr Clara B. Wilpert, Director of the Museum of Ethnology, Basel

Juliane Stephan, New York

Most of the photographs in this book are unique documents. The important photographs by Maureen Bisilliat, Leni Riefenstahl and Malcolm S. Kirk aroused my interest in the subject and inspired me to work on this book. Special thanks are due to them. Prof. Claus Hansmann and his colleague Matthias Holzapfel have been a great help to me in the past two years with excellent photos from their art-history picture archives.

Two of the authors, Ferdinand Anton and Martin Saller, deserve special mention. Our many conversations always led to improvements in the work.

The photographs in the book have come from a large number of photographers. Tracing and contacting them all was a long and arduous task, which Susanne Lange and Ute Heek of Frederking & Thaler performed admirably and indefatigably.

My thanks also go to the editor, Barbara Rusch, and the production manager, Karlheinz Rau.

The above lines would not have been written if I had not met my publisher, Monika Thaler, two years ago through Dr Andreas Pöllinger. Her personal commitment, courage, dynamism and enthusiasm made the book possible. For her belief in it, my heartfelt thanks.

KARL GRÖNING

Index